Tear-Watered Blooms

Tear-Watered Blooms

A Story of Learning
the Gift of Dependence through Suffering

by Catherine Rackley

foreword by Cindy Finley

RESOURCE *Publications* • Eugene, Oregon

TEAR-WATERED BLOOMS
A Story of Learning the Gift of Dependence through Suffering

Resource Publications
An Imprint of Wipf and Stock Publishers
199 W. 8th Ave., Suite 3
Eugene, OR 97401

www.wipfandstock.com

PAPERBACK ISBN: 978-1-5326-9057-0
HARDCOVER ISBN: 978-1-5326-9058-7
EBOOK ISBN: 978-1-5326-9059-4

Unless Otherwise indicated, all Scriptures are from the ESV® Bible (The Holy Bible, English Standard Version®), copyright © 2001 by Crossway Bibles, a publishing ministry of Good News Publishers. Used by permission. All rights reserved.

Manufactured in the U.S.A.   DECEMBER 20, 2019

For Jesus. *Every word* is for your glory and pleasure.

And for William. You, my love, have taught me what steadfastness and sacrificial love look like.

And for Vada. My angel, your joy and large personality is sunshine to my soul.

"Praise be to the God and Father of our Lord Jesus Christ, the Father of compassion and the God of all comfort, who comforts us in all our troubles, so that we can comfort those in any trouble with the comfort we ourselves receive from God."

—2 CORINTHIANS 1:3-4 (NIV)

Contents

Foreword

Friend,

In 2009, my husband and I sat before a Ukrainian judge. She, alone, would determine if we would leave her chambers with a daughter or return her to the orphanage and fly back home to the six children we left in Charlottesville, VA. Every detail of our life was open to her scrutiny, and the criteria for passing her test was undefined. The best we could do was present our case, answer her questions and hope that the love we felt for this eight-year-old orphan would result in a favorable verdict. I felt exposed, raw and completely vulnerable.

There are situations in life when we *choose* vulnerability and others in which vulnerability is *uninvited*. This courtroom vulnerability was one that we chose when we said "Yes" to adoption. Catherine knows *chosen* vulnerability, but she also knows the vulnerability that is *uninvited*, the kind that comes with a diagnosis. Perhaps you, like Catherine, know that moment when the doctor says, "You have cancer" or "You'll never have children." And in that moment, you are exposed, raw and completely vulnerable.

Catherine knows vulnerability.

She knows the vulnerability of stepping from the position of nurse to that of patient.

She knows the vulnerability of trusting her deepest desires to the wisdom of her husband.

She knows the vulnerability of spoken prayers that seem to hit an impervious heaven regardless of how unceasingly they are offered.

She knows the vulnerability of trusting God, even when trusting him means relinquishing control and watering the seeds of all that you desire with hot salty tears.

In *Tear-Watered Blooms*, Catherine presents her vulnerability like an offering to you and to me.

I first met Catherine when she expressed interest in RiverCross, the ministry I lead. With RiverCross, we bring healing and hope to the world's vulnerable children through the power of story. We choose to walk into their uninvited vulnerability and work to see them rescued and protected. Over the years, Catherine has served alongside me communicating gratitude to those who partner with us and coordinating prayer for the ministry. The work that she does with me is incredibly valuable.

But as much as I treasure the work Catherine does, what I treasure most is . . . her.

This spring I met with Catherine in her lovely home. I had come to pray with her, and while we did pray, there was something about being with her that evening that gave me a sense of comfort. Her home was quiet, candles were lit, and Catherine was fully present. Not a cell phone in sight. I chose vulnerability and shared my story with her. Because all that she has been through, but even more . . . who she is, I knew that my vulnerability would be safe with her.

As you read *Tear-Watered Blooms*, you will have this sense as well. Catherine chooses to share her vulnerability with us. And because of this, you are safe with her. *Tear-Watered Blooms* is her beautiful story of seeds of vulnerability, heartache, and longing sown into the fertile soil of God sovereignty, grace and mercy.

As you turn the pages, you will be invited to join Catherine in this garden. You will sit with her in well-ordered rows with the sun on your back and your hands filled with rich soil. Your tears will mingle with hers as you grieve alongside her and perhaps consider your sorrow. You will marvel as you watch the seeds of her pain, longing and loss take root, grow tall and become beautiful blooms.

As you sit with Catherine in these rows of tear-watered blooms, I pray that just as Catherine has done, you will see and trust God's hand with your pain. I pray that you'll choose vulnerability, turn to God, share with a trusted friend or two the longing you are experiencing, and begin your own sowing of tear watered blooms.

That day in 2009, waiting in the judge's chambers, I was exposed, raw and vulnerable. Our future, and this little girl's future rested in the hands of that Ukrainian judge. She heard about our family, questioned our intent (Did we plan to harvest her organs?), examined the pictures of our home and the room we had set up for this little girl. Eventually she turned to that little girl and asked a question no child should ever have to answer. "Do you want to be adopted by this family?" In that moment, it seemed like all heaven held its breath. And with barely a pause, this courageous eight-year-old looked the judge in the eye and simply said, "Da."

The months of watering the seeds of longing, conviction and all the trials of adoption bloomed that day as this child became our daughter. She became our tear watered bloom.

And now, my friend, may I encourage you to fix a cup of tea, light a candle, and turn the pages of *Tear-Watered Blooms*.

Blessings to you,
Cindy Finley

Acknowledgements

To the team at Wipf and Stock, thank you for believing that this story is worth sharing. Thank you for working tirelessly to bring it to print. Thank you for helping me share my story with others in an effort to comfort them and bring glory to Jesus' great name.

To Matt Mikalatos, thank you for your encouragement in the editing process. Thank you for making me a better writer. Thank you for believing in this story and for pushing me to the hard places in my heart that I didn't even realize I was resisting going to. You have helped me learn to be a more honest writer.

To Myrlande and Jennifer, my dear friends, both of you have undone me. You love well and deep and wide. Your humor and tears and prayers and constant presence are life to my soul. You teach me what faithful friendship looks like. You love when it's not easy or convenient. I am so thankful for you both and the ways you have taught me as your hearts blaze for Him.

To Abigail and Macon, thank you for being generous with your incredibly raw stories. Thank you for meeting one-on-one with me to help me process and look to Jesus, who alone satisfies the deepest longings of our hearts. Thank you for showing me that God really does bring beauty from ashes, when my heart was too sick to believe that. You have both mothered me in ways you may never know.

To Sara Hagerty and Katie Davis Majors, I'm not sure you will ever see these words, but your vulnerability in your writings were my inspiration for this book. You have no idea how much the Lord has used you in my life. I am deeply grateful for your efforts in making your books come to life. They have ministered to my soul and drawn the eyes of my heart Heavenward time and time again. You have ministered to me more than you will likely ever know.

To Cindy Finley, you stepped into my life when I was hungry for meaningful work in my life. Thank you for constantly reminding me of the power of God's Word through your example. You are a mentor to me, and a treasure in my life. I am so inspired and encouraged by your passion to follow Jesus anywhere he leads. Thank you for teaching me about trusting Jesus and doing work with excellence with your example in how you lead Rivercross. You are a gift.

To my precious friends, Kelly, Erin, Katie, Kristina, Angela, your phone calls and perfectly timed texts of encouragement light up my day. Thank you for your faithfulness in friendship through life's trials and joys. I love our times laughing together, and our times of crying on each other's shoulders. You are precious to me, and I thank God for you.

To Gemma Elizabeth Sunday, you are a jewel, sweet girl. You have grown into a beautiful, God-fearing, Steel Magnolia woman. I am so proud of you. You teach me how to persevere under tremendous trials that seem so unfair. Your grit, faith, humor, and integrity inspire me everyday. Thank you for your cheerfulness. I know we live an ocean apart, but you will always be a dear member of our family.

To Harold and Debra, how did I get in-laws like you? Thank you for teaching me to pray without ceasing. Your love for the unreached people of India inspires me and makes me want to live intentionally, as you are living. Thank you, Debra, for traveling with me to Ethiopia. Your presence on that trip was such a blessing. Thank you, Harold, for allowing her to go with me. Thank you for your constant support and love in our lives.

To Liz, my precious, big sister. You have always been so protective and nurturing to me. You love me hard. You are one of my biggest cheerleaders and I love being loved by you. How did I get you for a sister? You are one of my life's greatest gifts. Thank you for checking in on my heart with your big-sister-questions. I absolutely love living down the street from you and your crew. I love you.

To Mama and Daddy, your constant outflowing of love and generosity is such a beautiful reflection of Him. Daddy, you are my coach and one of my best friends. Thank you for always being so supportive and concerned. I love your adventurous spirit. I know that's where mine comes from. You are fun to be with. I love our coffee dates on Friday mornings. Mama, you love deeply. You have my back always, and I love that about you. Thank you for your constant support. You have taught me about not being in a rush, and how to take time for the people you love. In a world that screams "achieve and produce," you have taught me about "being" with others. I love that about you. I am so grateful for you both, and I love you both deeply.

To Vada, you are my heartbeat, sweet girl. I am so proud of you. Your enthusiasm for life, and deep affection for others teaches me every day about loving others well. Your active imagination and heartfelt giggles remind me to slow down and enjoy life's beautifully simple moments. I want you to know this story. I want you to look to the Lord in the dark hours of your life and trust that He is with you. He is the only one who can heal the very deepest holes of our hearts. He cares deeply for you. Thank you for your sunshine, sweet girl. The Lord is going to use you in mighty ways for his kingdom. You are his and Daddy's and my beloved treasure.

To William, you steady me with your quiet presence and constant support. Thank you for making our home full of laughter with your wit and silly antics. You are the reason I was able to write this book. You maintained life for us at home too many times to count, so that I could conquer this writing project. How do I say thank you for believing in this? You have been by my side through it all. You have endured these trials with honesty and faithfulness, and I see a deeper, richer faith in you because of them. We have walked, arm-in-arm through some violent storms and also seasons of unexplainable joy. You have taught me what honesty and faith look like woven together. You put my self-doubt at ease. Your deep love makes me love Jesus more, and for that I am so humbled and deeply grateful. I love you more than tongue can tell.

To Jesus, you are my heart's deepest longing. Life with you is fulfilling and rich. Thank you for the trials. Thank you for your gracious, larger-than-life presence, that has never moved or run away or even wanted to. Thank you for wanting a relationship with me, and pursuing it at all costs, even at the cost of seeing your daughter hurt. Knowing you is my life's greatest gift. Please don't let me waste my life. It is all for you.

Introduction

Life is unpredictable. And I like control. These are two realities that don't always mesh well. There are surprises that clothesline you, leaving you flat on your back gasping for air. I was laying on my back staring at the storm clouds looming overhead when I was told I had cancer and would need to undergo treatment that would include multiple chemotherapy drugs and radiation. Once that hit passed and I stood up again I was re-clotheslined when my husband was told that due to a congenital defect, he and I would never become pregnant "the old-fashioned way." Initially my husband and I were not on the same page about adoption, so I stayed down as I panicked at the potential of my two dreams of motherhood never coming true. I had barely gotten back on my feet when I was told that our beloved daughter, who was living in an orphanage over seven thousand miles away, would perhaps have to stay there until adulthood because Ethiopia passed a law to close international adoptions as we were in the middle of the process to get her. This caused a giant question mark to loom over the already very rocky process. I began questioning God's love, care and goodness to me as my heart lay bruised before him. I knew he could prevent it, fix it, and make all the bad go away. Why wouldn't he do that if he loves me?

We all have these experiences, these times of suffering, that we don't like. We desperately want them to go away, yet we are powerless to change our circumstances. Yet, somehow, I scramble, relentlessly, for it. These are the things that impact us, but it is Jesus who shapes us. We are not our experiences. We are *what we do* with our experiences. Have you ever had something blindside you? Something that seems so totally random? Something that feels unfair? I have just come out of a season of being blindsided multiple times in a row, each event being completely unrelated to the one preceding it. That is the premise for this book. Everything we have planned, practiced, coordinated, dreamed, and predicted can all be altered in just *one unexpected moment,* one sudden turn of events. Turns of events that are far beyond our control. It's these types of experiences that make a bad haircut or a wrong pizza delivery not such a big deal anymore. It's these types of experiences that bring perspective, flexibility, and (hopefully) a deeper faith. It's possible that a broken heart can fall into the mix too. It's these types of life experiences, ready or not, which bring wisdom. And . . . according to Proverbs 8:11 . . . wisdom "is better than jewels, and all that you may desire cannot compare with her." Is that true Lord? Because we are hurting. And we know you can make the hurting stop.

Wisdom comes with a price. Sometimes we don't want the experiences that build faith. Sometimes we don't want the experiences that cause us to wrestle in our understanding of who the Lord is and what his heart towards us is. But. But these are the things that have the potential to teach us. I am talking about the hard stuff. The stuff that pricks and stings. The stuff that's personal. The stuff that causes you close your eyes and wish for it to disappear (like now!). I hate cancer. I hate the monthly reminder that my womb is, and likely will forever be, empty. I hate that there are so many orphans living in horrible situations and it is so freaking hard to go through the adoption process, financially, emotionally, spiritually and otherwise. But experiencing each of these things has caused me to know Jesus in a different way than I did before. And for that, I am truly grateful. Could it be that these experiences are really gifts?

Sometimes the price of knowing Jesus more intimately and gaining wisdom is more than we are willing to pay. It was for me. But my willingness *didn't stop* the Lord from using hardship to teach me. And the lesson has been sweet. Preciously sweet. And undeniably difficult. Dependence is not learned through candy shop visits and sunny beach days. Could it be that our hardship is really his drastic pursuit of our affection? A door into an intimacy with the Lord that cannot be experienced by any other means? A reminder to number our days, and to love without boundaries because this world, with all of its messiness, is not our home. Are these hardships invitations to know our Father in a mesmerizingly beautiful way? A richer fellowship with the Lord is better than an easy day. My comfort and control of "my" day . . . those two things married together, I used to think (sometimes still do), make a really fantastic day. Sometimes we aren't offered those two things and we may kick and scream and pout and that's ok . . . for a time. But our kicking and screaming will only last for a time. Once our hearts are open to the Father, who is longing to hold us and kiss our foreheads in the midst of our distress, a spark of love ignites and the flame for him only grows the more we crawl into his lap. My heart has experienced the Lord in these ways. It is in these moments that my heart screams to my flesh, "better is one day in your courts, than a thousand elsewhere" Psalm 84:10. (NIV)

My prayer is that through this book, you will see your suffering differently. That you will see it as a bridge to the One who can comfort and love *you* like nothing or no one else. Sometimes our suffering is the only way to get to know him in this way. This intimately. So, my dear friend, know that your suffering is *not a waste*. It is an invitation into the lap of our eternal father who is longing to love you with an overwhelming abundance of generosity and tenderness and friendship and presence that you won't find anywhere else.

Your tears are watering the ground for a beautiful bloom that is coming in the spring. Maybe a whole garden of blooms. But, the biggest and most vibrant, of all those breathtakingly beautiful blooms is an intimacy with Jesus who is gently and tenderly reminding us to number our fragile days.

CHAPTER 1

A Bump in the Road

"The blacker the night around us grew, the brighter and truer and beautiful burned the word of God."

—CORRIE TEN BOOM[1]

It was January of 2013. My New Year's goals were in full swing. I had been married for three years to my husband, William. I was happy, carefree, and ready to change the world for Jesus. My zeal for the Lord was as fiery as ever. My optimism for life overflowed. My energy was high, and my passion was ablaze. Being a naturally optimistic person, my positivity was flowing much like sweet honey from a bustling beehive. Spending time with friends was my favorite thing to do. Many of us went to the same church and few of us had children. We were pouring into each other's lives with love, consistency, and open, flexible schedules. Our weekends were spent hiking, helping one another move from one-bedroom apartments into starter homes, eating out, splurging on dessert (that we could not afford), serving the community, and playing games, my personal favorite being Spades. My romantic, visionary self always overbidding, being the first to be eliminated because I had so many "bags." The sun seemed to be shining brightly. Relationships were easy and seemed to go deep almost effortlessly. I was happy.

1. Ten Boom. *Hiding Place*. 194.

As I lay in bed next to my sleeping husband, I rubbed the side of my right neck. "What is this lump?" I thought to myself. It wasn't tender to my touch or painful. Just some weird, benign cyst, I'm sure. It was only a matter of a few short months that it began to multiply. One lump turned into several lumps. Happening quickly, too. They slowly began to grow in size until they were no longer small. They started becoming noticeable to the people I was around. I couldn't just feel them anymore; I could see them when I looked in the mirror. Sitting at the dinner table at my in-laws' home, my father-in-law, Harold, asked me as I sat at the directly opposite side of the six person dinner table, "what is that bump in your neck . . . there, on the right side?" I vividly remember this moment, like a light bulb going off in my head. He can see that? I thought to myself.

After a few months passed with me trying to ignore these, what felt like, marbles in my neck, I decided to see a doctor. William had asked me multiple times to get it checked, but at the time, for whatever reason, it felt rational to wait and see if they went away on their own. As a nurse I would have never encouraged this sort of decision from one of my patients, but it made sense to me, somehow, at the time. The old saying that nurses make the worst patients is oh so true.

It was a normal working day at the hospital. I was assigned to be the nurse for one of the radiology procedure rooms. As a nurse in the radiology department, every week my position rotated between different areas of radiology and, thus, all different areas of the hospital. One week I might be in CT, then MRI, then interventional ultrasound, interventional CT and so on. The fact that I was assigned to this room, on this day, with this patient, for this procedure was no coincidence. The schedule was full and most of the procedures were going to be biopsies to check for suspected cancer concerns. In the department I worked in, most scheduled procedures were always "cancer rule outs." Scans were being done; biopsies were being taken to see if cancer was the criminal to be blamed for the patient's symptoms. Hindsight is so often twenty-twenty. I had an unnerving encounter with a patient I was prepping that day. God assigned me to *that shift, that room, that patient.*

She was a melanoma skin cancer survivor. She came to have a biopsy taken of a swollen lymph node . . . a swollen lymph node *in her neck.* The details of the scene are so vivid in my memory. I watched her as she lay on the exam table, patiently waiting to have the biopsy done. I nonchalantly rested my hand over my neck to feel the lumps there . . . just to confirm that they hadn't disappeared overnight. Nope, still there. My mind was starting to go down a road it hadn't gone before. What if this lump in my neck is cancer? No, it can't be, I reassured myself. Focus Catherine, you are at work. You can worry about that later. I prepped her for the procedure.

I could tell she was nervous. As she waited on the doctor, I could see her mind racing. She pulled at the neck of her gown, her fingers rising again to her neck, a mirror image of what I had just done myself a few moments before. I could feel the weight of this moment for her. I was beginning, for the first time, to feel afraid myself. Fear danced in her unsure eyes. Small talk was of no interest to her. Could I blame her? She wanted quiet. Compassion welled up inside of me. She may soon have to wage war with a cancer that had once been defeated. Something she had once defeated, so she thought, at no small cost. She had shed blood and sweat and tears, no doubt, over all of this once already. And here it was, returning to haunt her. Darkness loomed heavy in her heart. It filled the room. I was worried. What could this mean for her future? She waited in silence. I wanted to help her, but couldn't. No one could. My best gift of love was to honor her fears and pray. I stood quietly to the side against the wall, giving her the stillness that she was silently asking me for.

The heaviness in her heart served as a catalyst for me to consider that, even though I wasn't having her same symptoms, these knots in my neck needed attention. As we waited for the doctor, I could have prayed a thousand times. As most doctors often are, he was running behind schedule and I had ample time to be alone with my thoughts in the dimly lit procedure room. The knots in my neck were not supposed to be there. I had dealt with early stage melanomas as a child, just as this dear woman had a few short years earlier. Because of my divine patient assignment that day, the Lord led me to schedule the doctor appointment for myself that I should have scheduled months ago. God has a way of gently guiding and positioning us towards what is for our best. If we would only move forward. Trusting his provision. Because he *cares* for us. It was time for me to stop ignoring the mystery knots and get some answers. But answers don't always come as quickly as we would like. When we do get them, they aren't always the ones we want either.

A few days later I found myself scribbling my name on a form giving consent for the same procedure my patient had just had done. Soon I was being positioned on the top of a biopsy table. In what felt like just a blink of an eye, I went from being the one holding the patient's hand to being the one having my hand held. I felt scared. I felt unsure if I really wanted to know the answer while at the same time knowing I had to find out. I starred at the boring, white tiles that made up the room's ceiling while my mind raced with a million what if's and simultaneously coached myself off the mental ledge. I smoothed over my gown with my hands in an effort to try and maintain some sort of order to this moment that felt like chaos. Both comfort and control felt far away. I laid on the table top and prayed. I knew that I wasn't in control of the answer to this moment and hated that feeling. Turn your head to the left and try to relax, the doctor told me. The long, thin needle was inserted into my neck. He moved it back and forth vigorously trying to obtain enough cells on the needle by creating friction. I closed my eyes, cringed and endured the short-lived pain. He went away to look at the needle under a microscope and I waited, remaining on the exam table. He reported the first "pass" didn't give him what he needed. He did it again. And then again. After three passes with the biopsies not providing enough cells to see under the magnification of the microscope, I was scheduled to have the lymph nodes surgically removed in the operating room. It was still going to be an outpatient procedure, except under general anesthesia this time. I went home and was again left alone with my own thoughts as I prepared myself to go back to the hospital a few days later to have the procedure done that would surely give the diagnostics team what they needed this time. A twenty-four-hour day felt like a year as I waited and wondered. I felt a sense of relief when the day finally arrived for me to go back to the hospital. I went into the pre-op area. My Uncle Millard came to sit with my mom and dad during the operation. William's cousin came and sat with him in the waiting room. William was antsy, I could tell as I waited for the door to open and hear my name called to go back. I was prepped, my IV was started, I had an adorable little hair net on, and a mask was put to my mouth as I was instructed to count backwards from ten. I made it to seven when my eyes drifted off into a deep sleep and the bright lights of the operating room were the last thing I remember. The procedure was quick. The biggest lymph node was removed and sent to the lab. At this point, there were probably ten I could feel in my right neck, nine after the surgery.

I was quickly back to work a couple of days later and waiting to hear the results. Again, sitting in life's waiting room. The waiting room of life, short or long, is a hard room to spend time in. Life brings with it unexpected twists and turns, yet the world keeps turning and responsibilities don't stop. Have you ever wanted to hit a pause button on life, just so you could have time to process what was happening? I wanted to have a chance to make myself believe that this was really real. Or maybe, in truth, I wanted to hit the pause button to enjoy not worrying over what the answer might be. Frustratingly enough, there is no pause button. I've searched the remote control of life up and down; it is simply not there. We know the news we wait to hear shapes our future.

The Lord knowing the future is only a comfort when we also believe (alongside that) that he loves us. His sovereignty apart from his goodness is terribly scary. But his sovereignty cannot be divorced from his goodness. They are permanently welded to one another. *That* is one of the load bearing pillars of his great comforts to us.

Several days passed since my procedure in the operating room and I still hadn't heard from the doctor. I finished my shift and began the long walk to my car. I was lost in my own thoughts. What if this is cancer? Where is it in my body? How fast is it spreading? I would wake up in the morning wondering what had been silently happening inside of my body as I lay in bed resting. But I feel strong. No, it can't be. I would feel badly, right? Wouldn't I? What if it's melanoma? That's going to be bad. What if it's breast cancer? What if I have to lose both of my breasts? I spent a lot of time here. I began realizing how much a part of my womanhood my breasts made me feel. I developed a new-found compassion for the women I saw walking through this loss. I see-sawed between worrying about what "it" could be and also trying to "not go there" in my mind. On the "I'm not going there today" days I rationalized with myself. I coached myself asking, what good will speculation do? Why worry, Catherine, it may be nothing and you will have worked yourself into a frenzy over nothing. That "I'll cross that bridge if (and when) I come to it" mentality. It helps to combat the paralysis that links arms with anxiety. I preferred these days, but my emotional bank account was bleeding out. I was in the red. My mind and even my heart believed that God would give me grace no matter what was lying around the corner, but regardless, I was afraid.

The unknown is a scary place to be. It begs for faith. Rubber meets the road type faith. Not faith in the future. The future can bring with it fiery trials. The future can be terrifying, especially if we knew in advance what it holds for us. *But faith . . . . faith in the One* who knows the future. The One who knows the future *and also loves us.* The One who owns and holds the future, and *holds us.* It's a hard balance. Trusting God with the future, but also being wise to consider the implications of what may be lying ahead. Spending time preparing our minds and hearts for the things that may be coming while remaining grounded in God's sovereignty and goodness towards us in all things. I know you can relate. His arms are where I want to wait in these types of moments. These moments that life brings. His arms are warm and feel safer and more personal than the sterile, metal chairs sitting under the florescent lights of life's waiting room. And our hearts can be calm and peace filled, full of life even in the midst of an unknown future. My heart repeatedly tries to get up and walk out of his arms and back to the sterile waiting room, and sometimes I do, but he gently puts his hand on the small of my back and guides me back to his arms. He has me. He has you too. It's okay if you get up and try to leave sometimes. He won't let you go. He's like that.

I didn't think the doctor would have the test results when I called, but I was tired of waiting, annoyed even at this point. I had to find something out. I was getting antsy. I have been told that I can be an impulsive person. And impulsivity is not often a positive trait to be bent towards. It usually carries regret in a close tow. But I didn't care about that, I called. Concerns of breast cancer or melanoma loomed, but, deep down, I felt like I didn't know what in the heck I was going to be told. I felt open minded in the most out of control way. My heart pounded in an overpowering way. I could hear the "thump" of my heart ringing in my ears as I listened to the phone ring to the surgeon's office. I began to breath more quickly and I felt both so ready and so hesitant to know the answer all at the same time. Other than the swollen lymph nodes, I felt healthy. Active. Young.

Each of us who has had cancer, discovers it and wages war against it uniquely. No two battles are ever exactly the same. And cancer is *always* a war. For those who have never had it (and I pray as I write this, never will) you can understand this from the loved ones you have witnessed climb that mountain, or maybe plummet to the bottom in its defeat. It's a mountain layered with cliffs of fear, rocky ledges filled with pain, and steep valleys of discouragement.

The office nurse answered the phone as I cut through the hospital cafeteria to the street that led towards the car parking deck. Oh no, I thought. Someone actually answered, maybe he won't have the results in. I don't want to know now I thought to myself. Wait, but I do. I do want to know. These were the thoughts racing through my head. When I heard his voice on the other line of the phone he immediately and bluntly told me that I had something called Hodgkin's Lymphoma. Lymphoma? Huh? Did I hear you right? When I asked him about the details of this cancer, he said that I should "Google it." He told me I could learn more after he referred me to my oncologist. Taken back by his stoicism and this new diagnosis, I was silent on the other line. I had been warned by coworkers of this doctor's lack of bedside manner, but I was dumbfounded by his insensitivity. Our phone conversation was two minutes at best. When we hung up the phone, I continued the long walk to my car. I had an answer, but it wasn't the one that I had hoped for. It felt surreal. I had prayed. I had had faith. I believed he could have made this not so. But cancer it was. I watched the pedestrians around me. I felt like I was dragging my heart behind my body like a torn and tattered parachute. People talking on their cell phones, others busily rushing to and from work, hospital staff taking smoke breaks on the sidewalk, parents hurrying home to their beloved children. Car horns beeping in the background. My senses seemed to intensify and my breathing became heavy. My stomach hurt. I felt alone. The world kept turning, none of the strangers around me knew that I had just found out I had cancer. I didn't want their pity. It just felt surreal to learn news that was so bad in the middle of a world that was so unaware.

We never know what a person may be going through, do we? A reminder that, that moment on the bustling sidewalk, branded on my heart. A reminder that I need frequently. Maybe we got cut off in traffic because the driver was lost in his prayers for his wayward child. Maybe the snippy grocery clerk learned that she didn't get the university scholarship that was her hope for a higher education and a different job. Maybe the ungrateful homeless woman has been burned by so many people in her past she doesn't even know how to recognize an act of kindness. This world is *full* of hard days, and our hard scenarios are so very different from one another. We, *together*, are a broken people. The more grace we can show to one another, giving each other the benefit of the doubt because we so often don't know the details of each other's burdens, the more we will be aligning our hearts with the heart of Jesus. *The kindest giver of all time.*

It's amazing how a two-minute conversation can impact you so much. I looked at the faces of the people quickly moving up and down the busy sidewalk. I continued in shock. I am only twenty-five years old, I thought. The world kept a brisk pace. My steps were heavy and slow, and I held back the tears. I didn't talk to anyone right away. My childhood best friend, Erin, called me as I began driving home, but I couldn't answer. I desperately wanted to, but I knew if I did, I would tell her the news. There is no way I could have kept it from her. I felt that William should be the first to know, but I knew he was in a meeting at work, and I decided to wait to speak to him before telling anyone else. What is Hodgkin's Lymphoma anyway? All I knew was that I was getting a referral to a hematologic oncologist. From my nursing terminology class in college, I knew that hematologic meant "blood." I had a type of blood cancer. About half way home, I called William. "Can you come home?"

CHAPTER 2

Gasoline

"The scars whisper of his glory. The scars mean we are growing, and the biggest scars prove his faithfulness all the more."

—KATIE DAVIS MAJORS[1]

For some, a pre-cancer diagnosis may be traumatic, like an unmistakable bleed, an intense abdominal pain or horrible migraines. For others, it comes as a complete shock, blindsiding them. I think of the man who has a chest X-ray because of a simple cough, only to learn that he has stage three lung cancer. Or the mother of four who believes her fatigue is due to lack of sleep, only to learn she has ovarian cancer that is quickly progressing. Or the people, similar to my own experience, who have the cancer come on very subtly. Deceptively so. There is a symptom that is present but seemingly non-problematic. *My point is, each of our cancer journeys are so uniquely different from one another, and it is so important that we honor each person's journey.* Despite our unique differences though, I know we have a bond. A special compassion and tender understanding as we look on one another's pain, on one another's fears. As we remember what it felt like to watch our hair fall out and our energy steadily drain. As we identify with one another's discouragement. As we lock arms and lean into another's hope for healing. And that, my dear friend, is precious to me. If you or a loved one is walking down this road right now, my hope is that in

1. Majors. *Daring to Hope.* 95.

9

my sharing my cancer story with you, you feel a sister cheering you on the good days and sitting quietly at your bedside on your hard days.

I took a weekend getaway trip a few days after my cancer diagnosis. I spent the majority of the weekend outside, savoring the fresh mountain air with my family as I soared down the ski slopes. I appreciated my capabilities this time, in a new way. More than I had in the past. Life is frail, even for youth, I was realizing. We often feel invincible. Unstoppable. Youth or not, it's in our nature. Hard reminders make me squirm while also causing me to regain perspective. To remember the things that matter. They are a reset. A detox of the heart. From what I had been told by my doctor, my future would be full of many difficult days. Chemo would start as soon as I got home.

And it did. The chemotherapy did start. Every other week. It's one thing to be told this is what you are doing to do, it's quite the other to do it. Sitting on the exam table at my first visit to the oncologist's office after the diagnosis, she told me what I could expect. I listened to her explain the drugs I would be given and the list of (most common) side effects that accompanied each one. The list was long. I wasn't sure what to think as she talked. I wonder if I'll be nauseous, I thought? Have insomnia? Stomach aches? I wonder if I'll beat this? She kept talking. One main question still loomed in my head, but I was too afraid to ask. I didn't have to, I zoned back into the conversation when I heard her say it: "egg freezing." I began crying. Not primarily because I had cancer or because of the chemo that was waiting for me, but because this diagnosis meant a minimum of three years before we could start trying to have babies, and she was talking about egg freezing because "you just never know what drugs with these kinds of harsh side effects can do to your reproductive system." We were just about to start trying, I wanted to yell at her, knowing she was just the messenger but feeling angry at her nonetheless. I had been excited about that. I was excited about thoughts of pregnancy, having a baby, and for the dream of adopting children, something I had told William I would like to do. I felt angry that cancer was going to delay my dreams of biological or adopted children for several years, at least. You can't begin those types of major life events when you are sick. And there are strict rules in both the pregnancy and adoption world around growing your family after having cancer. Most people say a minimum of three to five years has to pass, cancer free that is, before even considering such a thing. Little did I know what lay ahead.

As I sat on the exam table, processing the reality of my dreams of children being delayed, I thought about how when I was young, I fantasized of being a mother to biological and adopted children. I would think about the ways that I wanted to love and inspire my children. To train them to be kind, fight for justice, and lead the next generation. Cancer delayed those dreams for me. At the time, I believed them to be delayed for the next few years only. Unfulfilled longings are, in their own way, the hardest of all challenges to endure. Little did I know at that time . . . this delay would be longer than three years. It would potentially be a lifetime if the Lord didn't do a work in our hearts and/or bodies. But in that doctor's office, a few years was a hard enough pill to swallow. It was what I could (barely) bear for that time. And at that time, it was enough.

What they had warned about with chemotherapy was right. Each week I would start to feel better from the last round of intravenous gasoline (I'm being facetious, of course, but a more accurate description if you ask me), and then, before I knew it, I would be going back for the next dose. My positivity faded quickly because I was so surprised by the pain I had in my mouth. No one warned me of this side effect. I remember waking up the morning after my first round of chemotherapy, and my mouth hurt so badly. I couldn't talk because it hurt too badly to move my jaws. This was not one of the side effects the doctor had warned me about. I couldn't fully close my mouth. The only way I could bear the pain was to sit, mouth slightly ajar, causing drool to occasionally fall from my lips. Swallowing hurt, because it caused movement. Not talking is very unusual for me. My nickname was "Chirp" growing up, because I can usually shoot the breeze with a tree stump (a personality trait I get from my uber outgoing father). I had not prepared myself mentally for this. I didn't know I needed to!

Popsicles became my closest companion. I felt like a five year old again, with a permanently stained red upper lip (strawberry flavored was my jam). You can try to prepare for the mishaps and disappointments that are inevitable in life, but so often we don't even know they are coming. Just like my mouth pain after chemotherapy, life can bring events, people, and pain that we didn't know were coming. Jesus says, "In this world you will have trouble. But take heart! I have overcome the world." John 16:33 (NIV). This verse took on a new meaning to me. I read it as my jaws throbbed and my gums ached. Will he overcome my mouth pain? I thought to myself.

William, my quieter husband, felt the discouragement of my silence. He said the house was so quiet without me chattering to him about things on my heart, dreams for the future, the dealings of the day. He has always teased that I talk a lot. That I have a "running list" of things in my head to tell him, and the list never seems to end. I even talk in my sleep. I now know he likes it, because when I was so quiet, he hated it. Truthfully though, the forced quietness was good for me. The Lord used that to teach me a lesson about the beauty and wisdom that can be found in the quiet moments. Proverbs 10:19 says,

"When words are many, transgression is not lacking, but whoever restrains his lips is prudent."

Well, I didn't restrain my lips, but he did for me. There is intimacy, I learned, that can be found in sitting quietly at his feet, with my mouth shut, listening. Although I wish I could have learned to be a better listener and comfortable with quietness without my mouth having to hurt like that. I know now, that my mouth pain changed my heart for the better in that way. I still like to talk, don't get me wrong. But I am more cognizant of my mindless chatter and my personal insecurities I had with the quiet. I'm more aware of the wisdom found in listening. There is something special about it, rare even. Jesus was a really good listener.

I remember an elderly woman who was on the same chemo schedule that I was. My treatment took several hours and so did hers. We would both sit in our recliners with lines coming out of our arms, and the chemotherapy running into our veins. We knew those drugs were both saving us and destroying us. I felt a strange connection to that elderly woman, especially since we never even talked. We would occasionally make eye contact with one another and offer a shy grin and head nod, as if to say "hello over there, I see you." We were facing each other, but separated by a wide hallway. She and her husband had a lot of years under their belt. The type of cancer I had was receptive to treatment and had a high cure rate. I never asked about her outlook. That's a hard question to formulate, even though I thought about it. There was a big age gap between us. It bothered me, seeing her get that chemo. I imagine she and her husband, if that's who he was, had spent most of their lives together. And here they were, fighting to preserve a few more. One more Thanksgiving, one more Christmas with their children and grandchildren. Time started looking more and more like a gift. A gift that I shouldn't take for granted. A gift that won't always be available. Life is brief. And we only get one. I was realizing that the people in our lives, the relationships, those are the things that are the scariest to think about losing. When you get sick, you think about how your life *really is* going to end one day. It's a guarantee. I was thinking about leaving the people I loved the most. That is the hardest part about cancer, I think. It stings. You don't want to leave the people you love. You don't want to miss out on their lives, their celebrations, their achievements, their sufferings even. The thought of being apart caused an intense ache to begin in my chest. These are the kinds of thoughts that force a surrender of your desires. A surrendering of the people you love most dearly to the Lord's tender care. You are forced to choose to trust that the Lord will be there for the people you love when you are gone and cannot. It's a lesson in dependence. A lesson in faith. These people that I was afraid of leaving and missing when I got sick—these are the very people who took care of me when I was ill.

William, our families, my friends, they bore my burden. They carried my load. They didn't realize it, I didn't either at the time, but they were my teachers, and I was their student. I quietly noticed the many ways they took care of me and did things that were thoughtful and helpful and kind. My best friend, Jennifer, arranged a meal train. Because of this "train" we would have dinner dropped off to us the day I got chemo, which was always on a Thursday, and for several days following the treatment. As if that were not generous enough, they would also bring a second frozen meal so that we would be well stocked, even on the days I felt well. Something that Jennifer requested they do, because, well, she didn't want me in the kitchen. For four months, I barely cooked one time. The practical love and generous spirit shown to us through these meals was so touching. Cards filled with loving encouragement and restaurant and shopping gift cards filled our mailbox, almost daily. I am so touched as I write this and remember those acts of thoughtfulness. My dear friend from nursing school, Shannon, drove from out of state one day just to go to chemo with me, then she took me out for a pedicure afterwards before making the long trip home. My childhood best friend, Erin, went with me to my first day of radiation because William had to be in Las Vegas for a business trip and she didn't want me to be alone. It was her birthday that day. She spent it sitting in a hospital waiting room. Those memories ignite a feeling that the sun does when it breaks through the clouds. Its radiance causes me to close my eyes and soak in the warmth penetrating my skin. Its warm presence can make the faintest heart grin. These memories I will treasure and try to implement with others for the rest of my life.

He didn't only provide for us through others, but through himself. He can do the same for you. His presence is ultimate. Sometimes we experience him through other people, sometimes through quite moments in his Word or nature. *We don't have to ask him to be the strength of our hearts, we can go ahead and thank him that he already is the strength of our hearts.* Psalm 73:26 says, "My flesh and my heart may fail, but God is the strength of my heart and my portion forever." He is strong enough to carry your burden for you. "The Lord is my portion', says my soul, 'therefore, I will hope in him." Lamentations 3:24

There is nothing sexy about chemotherapy. As in. Nada. nuttin'. Waking your newlywed husband up during the night because your stomach hurts doesn't exactly "set the mood." Honey, just dim the lights and bring me some more hemorrhoid cream on your way over. Also, can you pick up some more stool softeners on your way home? I'm out again . . . dern' constipation. He was good to me. When abdominal cramps would wake me in the middle of the night, he would wake up with me, hold me in his arms, and rock me, like you would rock a child, until I fell back asleep. I kept my head covered when we were at home, so he did too; something I began to realize he was doing several months in (he never wore baseball hats that much, especially inside the house). Ball caps and pajama pants looked good on him as he sat in his recliner piddling on the computer. He reminded me of how pretty he thought I was, truly causing me to never once doubt if he thought I was beautiful as a cancer patient. Him making me feel beautiful meant a lot because chemotherapy can make you feel so unwomanly. To feel weak and have stomach pains and mouth pain and be bald doesn't exactly make you feel attractive. But he did. I'm thankful for that. He made roughly one thousand trips to Jimmy John's (thankfully it was just around the corner from our then home) to pick up a cherry coke and barbecue chips, a craving I still can't explain. He took care of me when I was hurting, but little did I realize at the time how much he was hurting, too.

Watching your spouse suffer and being powerless to change the circumstances is a painful angle. Especially for the men in our lives who have a God-given instinct to protect. I dealt with the emotional and spiritual struggle during the diagnosis and treatment. William dealt with it afterward. He was strong for me when I needed him most. I was strong for him when he needed me later. Some things are outside of our control and outside of our protection. We all experience these things in life. That's when William had to realize that *I was in God's hands.* I was his wife, but more than that, I was God's daughter . . . .and he was God's son. And God is the only unchanging factor in our relationship. We will not always be together.

One of us will pass, likely before the other, but God is our immortal rock. That was something he was going to have wrestle through with God, one-on-one. The wrestling match lasted for a while. It took time. I watched and prayed. Thankfully, God did not let William or I out of his grip when things got tense.

It's strange, the things that we believe we are in control of. The things that we plan out in our lives with such believed "certainty." I think that I am in control over my body, and, in some ways I am. I decide what food I put in my mouth. I decide what pills I am or am not going to take. I decide whether I will work out or stay on the couch. I decide if I will follow a doctor's recommended treatment plan or not. I decide what time I will go to bed. But total control is an illusion, I've learned. It's taken a few hard hits for me to grasp this. And there may be more in my future . . . likely so. What I know is that I can press *into a God who is in control*. He has my good at heart. A belief that he would tenderly remind me of in the darker days that lie ahead. Do you believe God has your good at heart? It's a hard question to ponder when there is a storm raging overhead. Don't shy away from considering it though. We serve a God who is really good at considering "the hard stuff" with us. He won't condemn you for your questions. He'll show you the answers. Maybe now . . . maybe later.

CHAPTER 3

I'm a Nurse, I'm a Patient

"Be strong and courageous. Do not be frightened and do not be dismayed, for
the Lord your God is with you wherever you go."

—JOSHUA 1:9

During these first weeks of treatment, I realized an undeniable act of
God in my life. I realized that *he knew* I was going to be sick and need treatment. *He placed* me at Duke Hospital to work even though he knew how
intimidated I am by large institutions. *He knew* I would soon be a patient
there, not just an employee. Where has God, in his loving care, placed you?
Is there a calling *you* have been resisting because it's unconventional, or
counter cultural or "unwise" according to your financial advisor? Go. Do it.
Follow his leading, even if you are scared.

He has plans for *you*. You are where you are or where he is telling to
go on purpose. *His goodness is woven into your small decisions of obedience.*
God placing me at Duke allowed me to be familiar with the facility, which
made me feel much more at ease going through the treatment. Knowing
the ropes of the cancer center lessened my anxieties. I knew the logistics
for my treatment at Duke. That allowed me to save my energy for the emotional difficulties that lie ahead. God's gracious provision to me envelops
those memories. What ways can you look back on your past and see God's
tender kindnesses to you? His provisions that you didn't even know that
you needed. His maternal like thoughtfulness over your needs you didn't

even know you would have. *He doesn't just supply our needs, he does it in a wooing, nurturing way.* He doesn't just love us out of duty. He doesn't love us because he is supposed to. He goes over and beyond because he is romantic like that. We are precious to him. He tucks a love note in our travel bag. He puts his hand on the small of our backs and gently directs our path. He grins at us while he leans in to whisper his ways in our ears. His nudging is our good. "The heart of man plans his way, but the Lord establishes his steps" Proverbs 16:9.

As a new nurse, I was afraid that I wasn't smart enough to care for the types of patients that had to go to Duke Hospital. They see some of the sickest of the sick. I was far from the brightest student in my class. The fear of failure loomed. This is an area the Lord has tenderly grown me in over the past several years. I was diagnosed with cancer a year after I decided to take this, what felt like, out-of-my-league nursing job. Is the Lord calling you to a place that intimidates you? To a role you don't feel qualified for? To a phone call that you are scared of making? If the call is clear, *go.* There is a reason he is calling to you. It may be scary, but his peace will be your close companion. That peace is worth a lot. I remember an unmistakable confidence when I made the decision to accept employment at this world-renowned medical center. A confidence that surprised me since I am more of a small environment type of person. That unmistakable peace was God. Fear is not the enemy. Not having the courage to walk forward in faith, when we are afraid, *that* is the enemy. I was not extended an offer after my first interview. I felt so strongly that I was supposed to be working at Duke, though. I held onto the hiring manager's business card. I typically throw everything away. I am a minimalist that thrives on simplicity and organization. Not throwing her business card away was very unlike me, but a nagging inside made me decide to keep it. A nudging I had in my heart. A few weeks later she called me with a job offer. Have you experienced those unexplainable leadings from the Lord before? It may be something small, but those things matter. It's easy to look back and have our faith built up as we begin putting puzzle pieces together and the picture is revealed. Some times that picture illuminates after a few weeks or years, other times it may never make sense. Or we may wonder, did I hear you wrong, Lord? We can hold on to the times when the picture does make sense, letting it build our faith for the times that it doesn't. I saw God's sovereign hand in my life with this Duke job, but there were things that lie ahead that I would not understand so easily.

Fast forward one year from being hired. Work was different now. As you can imagine, my relationship with my job changed dramatically. Work wasn't just work anymore. It became much more personal. Work was now the place that I had to go, if I wanted to get better. Life can shift our perspectives with no warning signs. This was the same cancer center that I had been caring for patients in as a nurse. Ironic, isn't it? Spending time in another's shoes makes empathy so much easier (one of the reasons I believe the Lord allows/appoints—dare I say appoints?—us to suffer). It was my turn now. My turn to have the scans done to my body, to lie on the exam table, to be poked and prodded, to be measured in every way possible. I had to check in at the front desk and wait for my name to be called by the nurses who would be caring for me, many of whom I had seen in the hospital cafeteria on my lunch breaks. I wasn't used to being on this side.

On my working days, I walked into the hospital with gratitude for the opportunity I got to care for others. I wanted to be strong and cheerful for them. On treatment days I walked into the hospital, with humility, fighting anxiety about the treatment side effects that I knew were lurking around the corner. I would feel afraid as I would think about patients from the shift I worked the day before, remembering the sadness in their eyes so clearly in my head. I would feel sad that some of them weren't getting better and afraid that I was going to follow in their footsteps. Walking into the cancer center for my morning shift felt heavy and different. I had to take a deep breath and tell myself "you can do this" every time I transitioned from being a patient to a nurse. There were many days I would get radiation on the first floor and walk up to the third floor to begin my shift. I would go to the bathroom first and make sure I scrubbed the marker off that told the staff where to radiate on my neck and arm before starting work. After I finished eight rounds of chemo, radiation began and lasted every day for three weeks. The team was cheerful and kind. They always seemed happy to see me. It made me feel good. It was a quick treatment, once I was on the table, not lasting even five minutes. I would get up, go to my little dressing room, put my scrubs on and of course my headscarf too. I would take my patient hat off and put my nursing hat on. Actually, that's a lie, my scarf always stayed on. I was insecure about a giant benign cyst that my hair used to cover. The Lord provided what I needed to both be a patient and to be a caregiver. He had called me, during that season to be both.

As the third week of radiation began, I began to get tired. The effects of the chemo were still lingering in my system and the accumulation of the radiation on top of that was causing a lot of fatigue. Chemo would knock me off my feet a day or two after getting it, but after three days I would feel okay again. Radiation was much more subtle in its approach. Slow and steadily over time, the accumulation in my body began taking me down a little bit more each day.

As I saw patients come in for scans, I began to feel guilty. Guilty that my treatment was working, and, many times, theirs were not. Why Lord? I would ask. Why am I getting better? I wanted to get better, but I wanted everyone there to get better too. Enduring chemo is too hard for it to not work. I will never forget a young, beautiful, strong, single mother that came in for a CT scan. She had two young children with her. She was a working woman, trying to provide for her little ones, even in the midst of her sickness. She was there because her cancer was back, and with a vengeance. I felt so sad as we talked. I wasn't responsible for children that needed me to tuck them in at night, help them with homework, read them stories, and fix their breakfast. My heart broke for this woman. I desperately wanted to trade places with her. I wanted her to be getting better, and me to be the one getting worse, if that's the way it has to be God. Does it, God? Her kids needed her there to pack their lunches and kiss their scraped knees. I didn't have any children. The tears I felt rolling down the vessels of my heart as we talked began to roll down my cheeks. I went into the bathroom and cried. The tears came like a flood. "Lord," I prayed, "heal her, Father, please. Heal her, I beg you. Jehovah Rappha, our healer, touch her cells with your mighty hand and make her well." With radiology nursing, you never know those you will cross paths with again and those you will not. Likely due to schedules that were not aligned, I never saw her again after that day. I hope and pray for her healing, even as I write this, not knowing the outcome of her story, or if her battle is maybe still going on?

Being on the patient's side of the fence felt vulnerable. It felt humbling. Cancer has a blunt way of reminding us of our own mortality. Spending time being the one receiving the care taught me things that nursing school never could have. Textbooks can't teach you ways to be sensitive to a person with fear in their heart. All night study sessions don't instruct you on the importance of small acts of kindness that can change a discouraged heart's day for the better. Textbooks didn't teach my nurse to bring me a warm blanket because she knew I liked that, or to turn on the music she knew I found comforting as I waited for my treatment. Textbooks didn't teach my radiation oncologist how to be friendly and kind when he knew his patients were suffering. I can see Dr. Kelsey's kind smile now as I type. Textbooks don't teach us to care for people tenderly, with empathy, affirming their value as human beings when they feel like lab rats. Straight A's don't measure your listening skills. Isn't that what Jesus does for us? *Comfort us. See beyond our skin and into our hearts.* He takes time for the little things that mean so much. When Jesus healed people. He healed with a word. It is a comfort to remember that our great physician needs no massive machinery to scan us in order to know where the disease lay, nor potent medications with vicious side effects for healing, nor baseline blood, heart, and lung tests to measure how well everything is functioning. *He needs none of that. Our great physician has all he needs on his very lips.* "He (Jesus) said to the paralytic—'I say to you rise, pick up your bed, and go home.' And he rose and immediately picked up his bed and went out before them all, so that they were all amazed and glorified God, saying, 'We never saw anything like this!'" Mark 2:10b-12

CHAPTER 4

Bye-Bye Hair

"This—all this mess—was fodder for discovering his love anew. Every single
dark day was an invitation."

—SARA HAGERTY[1]

It was a regular day at work. While in the restroom, I noticed something. My hair. My long strands of sandy brown hair scattered all throughout the bathroom floor. Wow, it looked like a wooly mammoth had been
at the barber in here. How many people have noticed this? I thought to
myself. In that moment I knew it was time. It was one thing for my hair to
be covering my pillow case each morning and clogging the shower drain,
but in public? At work? This is embarrassing.

My head had to be shaved. It had already gotten very thin. I asked
William to do it the next morning. It was a Saturday. He pulled out his
clippers and shaved my head. In some ways it felt freeing. In other ways it
felt humiliating. After he finished, we read Proverbs thirty-one together.
When reading verse thirty "Charm is deceitful, and beauty is vain, but a
woman who fears the LORD is to be praised" . . . it felt different this time.
I tied a scarf around my head and cried. I knew how much he loved my
hair. He always told me that. I loved it too. I thought of the line from the
movie *Little Women* when Amy says to Jo in disbelief after she sells her
hair to help her family, your one beauty Jo! How could you? I could relate.

1. Hagerty, *Every Bitter Thing*. 91.

My hair was always one of the few things that I really liked about myself. I tried to remind myself that it'll grow back. I was surprised at how attached I was to it. I fought to remember Proverbs thirty-one to keep my perspective Godward. *From where does our beauty really come?* This is the question I kept redirecting my heart to.

I know now that a woman's beauty does not merely come from her gorgeous, bouncy curls or her fresh highlights or cute layers. Truth be told, I knew that then too. But it's different having to flesh it out and believe it in your heart when you have a bald head shining back at you in the mirror. It took on a new meaning. God's word was a sweet reminder to me of what makes a woman beautiful. Isaiah 61:3 says, "to give them a beautiful head-dress instead of ashes, the oil of gladness instead of mourning, the garment of praise instead of a faint spirit; that they may be called oaks of righteousness, the planting of the Lord, that he may be glorified."

Now, looking in the mirror instead of noticing how my part wasn't right, I saw more of my soul, and I asked myself again, what is it that *really* makes a woman beautiful? A question, I dare say, many of us women would do well to ask ourselves more of. In a culture that glorifies the perfect exterior, we can so easily get swept away in the riptide of image. Superficiality can devour us. Rubbing my hand over my smooth, shiny head, I knew . . . I knew from Proverbs thirty-one, beauty is more than what TV, magazines, and my own insecurities tell me. And to my dear friend reading this, *your beauty is too.*

The Lord takes broken situations and makes wonder out of them, that he may be glorified. The Lord is enthralled with the beauty of a woman who trusts in him. 1 Peter 3:3-4 says, "Do not let your adorning be external-the braiding of hair and the putting on of gold jewelry, or the clothing your wear-but let your adorning be the hidden person of the heart with the imperishable beauty of a gentle and quiet spirit, which in God's sight is very precious." A spirit that wisely builds others up and does not tear down is beautiful. A beauty stemming from a unique ability to nurture others. To "mother" and "give life" to the people she is around, that's beauty. To be courageous rather than crippled when fear tries to overtake, that's beauty too. To be amenable when others are being disruptive. To be a peacemaker. To fight for her family. To fight for those who have no voice. *The softness and approachability of a dove, with the backbone of a lion.* Yes, a woman's beauty comes from her being a steel magnolia. No, I didn't need my hair to be beautiful. No woman needs that. Shaving my head that day was a flowing set of extensions for my heart.

CHAPTER 5

Why is This Happening?

"And I will put this third into the fire,
and refine them as one refines silver,
and test them as gold is tested.
They will call upon my name,
and I will answer them.
I will say, 'They are my people';
and they will say, 'The Lord is my God.'"

—ZECHARIAH 13:9

I sincerely believed that God had not abandoned me in this place. But why? Why was this happening? This is the question I would spend time mulling over in the quiet moments, the alone moments. In my heart *I knew* that the Lord is good, but I couldn't seem to make out the picture he was drawing. *And it hurt.* But *I knew* he was good. *But it hurt.* How do we reconcile truths that we know, with circumstances that seem to be ripping us to shreds? The pain is real. Our hearts feel like they have been caged with a saber-toothed tiger. We are standing before the Lord, ripped, shredded, and bloody, fighting to say out loud and continue believing what his Word says about him being our almighty, good, sovereign father and friend. How do we connect the dots between the reality of life with the riches of Christ? I am still learning the answer. Maybe that is part of what this Christian life is. Maybe that's what they mean . . . what Christ followers are always talking about, authentic *faith*. We don't like to suffer. And that's normal. But are we living entitled when we bark at God for not giving us the things we want? Or for giving us the things we don't want? I wonder if our view of suffering is wrong in America. An "I've got this" mentality culture that prides itself on independence, immediate gratification, and pulling yourself up by your own bootstraps. Suffering was making me face these questions in my own heart.

I met a trusted friend and mentor, Abigail, at Starbucks to discuss these thoughts. We had met there a hundred times for a midafternoon caffeine pick-me-up and conversation that always involved heart checks. She has a passion for women's bible study and discipleship. She had been mentoring me for years. I love meeting with her. She spent many years living in Brazil serving many different types of people including indigenous people groups. That, coupled with her insatiable appetite for God's Word, makes her perspective especially fresh and trusted. I'm deeply grateful for this friendship. She has walked through her fair share of difficulties and the Lord's love breathes out from her because she spends so much time worshipping him in solitude. She chooses her words carefully and isn't afraid to ask the hard questions. Walking into Starbucks we spotted an empty table and one of us snagged it while the other made her order. This Starbucks is a bustling one in one of the busiest sections of Raleigh and an empty table, especially one that feels semi tucked away where private conversation and prayer (always prayer with Abigail), can be like finding a golden egg at an Easter egg hunt. I jumped on it. Honestly, I am not a huge fan of Starbucks . . . I think their coffee is overpriced and kind of bitter, but somehow, I end up meeting people there often. I do mind paying for the name, that is, of course, unless it is during the Fall and I am ordering their five-dollar Pumpkin Spice Latte (insert eye roll emoji here). Five dollars, really? For a size small, excuse me, "tall" coffee? Am I the only one who does not understand their sizing name choices? I refuse to succumb to ordering from Starbucks using their sizing terminology. "So yes, I would like to please have a *s-m-a-l-l*, overpriced, (yet delicious) Pumpkin Spice Latte. A tall? No, a small." Anyway, I digress. But seriously, I am a total sucker for the deliciousness of that latte. Whew, I can taste it now as I write on this hot, North Carolina summer day. As I talked to Abigail about sin and Satan and the cancer, she suggested something that I was not expecting. Something bold. She proposed that maybe God not only allowed this cancer to happen, maybe he *ordained* it. Ordained my cancer?

Seriously? "Are you suggesting he chose this for me?" This did not go over well with me at the time. I felt a little edgy anyways but even so, I thought it was bold to suggest such a thing. She did it though, in her true friend style, with gentleness and a sincerity that is so true of who she is. But, gentleness or not, I didn't care. I left our coffee date that day peeved . . . yes at her, but mostly at God. Would God really do that? My anger flared inside me as I drove away in my car. I felt upset and confused. If she is right, how can a God that loves me choose to make me hurt? Why would he choose to make me sink low?

Later I would ask, with a greater sense of urgency and deeply hurt feelings, why would he delay the dream of motherhood for me? Why would he choose to make me a hypochondriac about all future aches, pains, bumps (after having cancer it is easy to get a headache and be convinced you have a brain tumor)? How can you do that to someone that you love? I would never do that to someone that I love, I thought to myself. Somehow, I had come to the place of being able to reconcile the idea of him allowing it to happen, but choosing it? No, that felt like too much. Angry or not, something small inside me immediately knew that maybe this thought was worth exploring. Maybe she was right. But in that moment, scoffing was easier than exploring. This idea hurt too much to explore. I thought God loved me. Does it bother him to see his children in pain? I was mad at him. I didn't want to talk to him. Cynicism felt easier than consideration. Maybe there was truth to be uncovered here. Maybe Abigail was right.

Dependence. This was the answer that I came to once I mustered the courage to pray through it. Maybe it wasn't actually me mustering the courage to pray. Maybe it was the Lord gently prying back the fingers of my heart that I was white knuckling before him. It came with the passing of time and with painfully honest prayers. Don't you love me, God? Isn't that what your Word says over and over? Why would you allow this? Why would you maybe even choose this for me? That hurts. I don't know if I can be in an intimate relationship with someone who chooses hurt for me. These are what my raw prayers looked like. And I meant them. I pouted. I yelled. I would sit before him, face down in my hands, and say "help me." Sometimes those were the only words I could get out. But I sought him. I sought to understand why he would (possibly) choose for me to experience pain. I sought to understand why he would choose and allow for me to experience pain when he had the power to stop it. Redirect it. I sought to understand why he would ordain this for me when he tells me over and over again in his Word that he loves me and I am special to him, his daughter. I began to open my mind and heart to him, once I was done fussing, and truly try to understand the why. I was asking him the hard questions. He both listened and answered.

Creating dependence is how you do that to someone you love. Not dependence in an egocentric, power tripping kind of way. Not dependence that he somehow needs. Dependence that breeds vulnerability. Dependence that breeds faith. From there vulnerability yields a new level of intimacy, and deeper the roots of faith weave into the ground. And I have come to realize that my "doing for the Lord" wasn't what he wanted from me. *He wanted me.* Unfiltered, alone, dependent, real . . . Enough with the all the "right answers" and being "gung-ho" to win the world for Christ. *He wanted me to sit with him in the quiet and just "be" together.* To quiet my heart and mind before him in the secret, like Jesus did. Luke 5:15-16 "But now even more the report about him (Jesus) went abroad, and great crowds gathered to hear him and to be healed of their infirmities. But he would withdraw to desolate places to pray."

This was a level of relationship that I wasn't looking for. He was. He wanted that with me. And this was one of the ways for our relationship to get there. He was willing to use sacrificing my physical health and my heart's desires to grow my spiritual health. My body may have been failing me, but though not what I wanted, my soul was beginning to have shoots of green sprout from dried, brown branches. I didn't realize it at the time, but I would later, and later (like way later) I was, well, thankful.

It seemed a little twisted, but it was also beginning to make more sense. *Was my suffering really God's compassion towards me?* Was this really him calling me? Was it one of the ways that he knew would create something deeper and bigger between my heart and his? Was he gifting me with himself? Was the only way for me to begin to understand the value of such a gift to come to the end of myself? Was dependence the key to receiving such an offer? He saw the big picture. He cared more about my soul than my comfort, control or happiness. *He was coming after me.* Was this hurt really love? Maybe my thoughts on love were superficial. Maybe my thoughts on love were cheap. On the surface it seemed twisted. I know God would never manipulate. That's not who he is. But the more I explored it, the more I sat in the quiet before him, things were beginning to make more sense. I started talking to him differently. I was spending time with him because my need felt so desperate. Time with him was essential. He never walked away when I screamed at him. He never left my side when I turned away from his comfort. He never accused me when I shook my fist at the ceiling. The spiritual realm is not one that I can see or touch. And it is certainly not the same message that our American culture banners. This was new.

Instinctively, the next question came . . . what was I going to do with it? Was I going to let bitterness harden my heart? Was I going to wallow in self-pity and stay angry at him? Faith. It's easy to say I have faith. It can be hard to live it. "A watching world might say, 'Why hope for life in a world of death?' And we know the answer. This world is not all there is, and death is not the end. Our fight is not for this life. Our fight is for eternity. And a hope for eternity truly cannot disappoint."[1] This is one of the beautiful gifts of suffering. It causes us to focus more on eternity. We begin to believe more that we really are just sojourners in this world. We are on our way home. We aren't home yet.

Experience breeds vulnerability. Where was I going to let this vulnerability take me? Down the path of bitterness, or down the path of dependence . . . looking to God for help in time of need? Was I going to choose to let it ruin my faith? Or was I going to look up to him in *faith*, asking him to strengthen it? Where are you? We all go through crisis. 1 Peter chapter one is a good place to park if you are struggling with these same questions right now. I know I find myself throwing the anchor of my soul back into this chapter a lot.

During my cancer journey, there was another passage that I went back to many times. It spoke to me. My cancer theme verses, if you will . . .

John 6:66-67, "After this many of his disciples turned back and no longer walked with him (Jesus). So Jesus said to the twelve (disciples), "'Do you want to go away as well?'" Simon Peter answered him, "'Lord, to whom shall we go? You have the words of eternal life, and we have believed, and have come to know, that you are the Holy One of God.'"

In this passage, many of Jesus' disciples turned away from him because they thought that his teaching was too harsh. When Jesus asked Peter if he was going to leave too, Peter basically said "where am I going to go if I do?" I love his honesty. His practicality. Once you have tasted the realness of God, even if it was only for a second, you know that there is no turning back. Experiencing God is too good. Peter had believed God. He had a relationship with him. He knew what he was like. He knew that he was good. I thought about this passage a lot when I had cancer. If I stop believing

---

1. Majors. *Daring to Hope.* 83.

Jesus, then what? *Where is there to go except his arms?* I really asked myself that question. I couldn't think of anywhere that would offer any kind of real, tangible, and lasting comfort. Everything else I experienced was like a bucket with a hole at the bottom. Not Jesus, though. He really could fill me. And in his arms I would often squirm and fight, and he would continue holding me, with a soft, patient, "It's ok my child" compassionate grin on his face. There I could sense his gentleness and his immense strength. And there in his arms his love felt tangible to me.

It's time to flesh this faith thing out. Within the first week of learning that I had cancer, William told me "this is where the rubber meets the road." He was referring to my faith. He said it black and white. A man of few words, straight to the point. There isn't a lot of grey with him. It seemed unnecessarily direct at the time, but I came to be grateful that he said it. I knew that he was right, and I thought about it many times when I felt angry at God or hurt by him. "God help me. God help me when I dread going in and having those chemo drugs burn my veins. God help me when I feel bloated and bald, and my peers look young and vibrant and beautiful. God help me as my friends tell me one after the other that they are pregnant and that dream feels so far away now that I'm sick. God help me when I want to go out and be active but don't have the energy. God help me when I stare longingly across the church sanctuary on Sunday at the family with multiple adopted children and wonder if cancer will prohibit me from being eligible to do this, God help me when I worry that this treatment isn't going to work and my husband is going to be left a twenty-three year old widower. God help me . . . " and he did. He does. He is still helping me. He is holding me in his grip. A loving grip that is so strong and faithful. My nimble fingers surely can't pry his fingers away. I am so grateful that he holds onto us and doesn't let go. 2 Timothy 2:13 says, "if we are faithless, he remains faithful—for he cannot deny himself." These reminders make my heart glad.

"So we do not lose heart. Though our outer self is wasting away, our inner self is being renewed day by day. For this light momentary affliction is preparing for us an eternal weight of glory beyond all comparison, as we look not to the things that are seen but to the things that are unseen. For the things that are seen are transient, but the things that are unseen are eternal." 2 Corinthians 4:16-18.

There is a story that speaks to the things we have been discussing in this chapter. There are few things that I find more beautiful than this story.

It encapsulates the purpose behind the pain the Lord allows, sometimes even ordains, in our lives. This story inspires me to endure, to believe the Lord, to fight the fight on Earth because of the reward that is coming later. I read this in a women's Bible study, a Bible study led by my aforementioned friend Abigail, that I did several years ago with a group of women . . .

"There's a familiar story in Christian circles about a group of women that met for a Bible study. While studying in the book of Malachi, chapter three, they came across verse three that says: 'he will sit as a refiner and purifier of silver.' This verse puzzled the women and they wondered how this statement applied to the character and nature of God. One of the women offered to find out more about the process of refining silver and to get back to the group at their next meeting. That week, the woman called a silversmith and made an appointment to watch him at work. She didn't mention anything about the reason for her interest beyond her curiosity about the process of refining silver. As she watched the silversmith, he held a piece of silver over the fire and let it heat up. He explained that in refining silver, one needed to hold the silver in the middle of the fire where the flames were the hottest, so as to burn away all of the impurities. The woman thought about God holding us in such a spot; then she thought again about the verse that says: 'he [sits] as a refiner and purifier of silver.' She asked the silversmith if it was true that he had to sit there in front of the fire the whole time the silver was being refined. The man answered yes, he not only had to sit there holding the silver in the fire, but he had to keep his eyes on the silver the entire time it was in the fire. If the silver was left a moment too long in the flames, it would be destroyed. The woman was silent for a moment. Then she asked the silversmith, 'How do you know when the silver is fully refined?' he smiled at her and answered, 'Oh, that's easy—-when I see my image reflected in the silver.'"[2]

2. Kassian and Demoss. *True Woman 201.* 128.

CHAPTER 6

The Value of Veggies

"God wants me to know the nearness of him in response to the deepest questions of my story, the kind of nearness that, when realized, heals."

—SARA HAGERTY[1]

With a scary cancer diagnosis comes a lifestyle evaluation. They are, in some ways, married to one another. Cancer made me question things in my life that I had never considered when I was healthy. One of those things was my nursing career. I had loved being a nurse, but all of the sudden I began to ask, am I really helping people get better? I like helping people. I think most of us do. But, suddenly, I was questioning the work that I was doing. Was I really helping? Or was I just reacting. I felt like I was not doing the proactive things that would benefit people the most. Our western medicine culture began to butt heads with the research I was doing about my cancer. I was in a tug-of-war between everything I had been taught and believed to be true and the things I was learning about. Things like nutrition, a plant-based diet, juicing, and detoxifying your body. This nursing job that I worked forty plus hours a week at, believed in with all of my heart, suddenly I was wondering if I was really making any difference at all. Is another pill really the answer? Another pill that has a thousand potential side effects, I thought to myself? Another medication that is going to require another medication to combat the side effects the first one brings. I felt

1. Hagerty. *Every Bitter Thing*. 107.

confused about something I had never felt confused about, my job. It began to feel less fulfilling. It was disillusioning.

This newly discovered quest for health began as I was working in the radiology department at Duke Hospital. An older patient, with a big smile, cheerful, rosy cheeks, and a face I can see, yet a name I cannot remember (nor I would be allowed to share it here because of patient privacy laws anyway), saw the scarf around my head and asked me if I shaved my head to support the patients. I took note of his baseball-cap-covered-head, and continued wiping his arm with the alcohol swab I had pulled from my scrub pocket. I didn't look at his eyes but internally, I was slightly taken back by his question. My knee jerk response at the time was to say something snarky, but instead I politely answered that I too, was being treated for cancer, as I carefully examined the vein in his arm that I had chosen for his IV sight. A conversation ensued that involved him telling me about a documentary called, "Forks over Knives." This documentary changed my life, he told me with a wink and a big, cheerful, happy to share grin. He said it with conviction . . . unapologetic belief and a joy that made me curious. His confidence in this remedy and his own personal testimony about it hooked me. He had had cancer and he had found an empowering way to fight it and he wanted to share that. That's cool, I said, what's it about?

Naturally, as a fellow cancer patient, I was intrigued by his passion on this topic. I mean, he was speaking from experience, right? I finished starting his IV, led him to the scanner, and made sure he got positioned comfortably and correctly on the table. I wrote down the name of the documentary, shoved the paper into my scrub pocket and continued on with my shift. He gave me a head nod, a confident grin, and another wink as I walked away from him, slightly puzzled by his cheerfulness on the topic and totally intrigued at the same time. I wanted to go home right then to see what my new friend found so mesmerizing about this documentary. Why was it so compelling? Life changing? That's strong verbiage. I wanted something to change my life. He was so positive and upbeat. His eyes had lit up as he had shared this information with me. I thought about our conversation throughout the remainder of my shift. I check checking my wrist to see if my watch would tell me I could go home now. Once it finally did, I immediately went home to check it out. I wanted the reigns of my health back in my hands. I was grasping, desperately, for control. Isn't control what we all want?

I watched the documentary that night. I didn't realize it would affect me the same way it affected him, but it did. A spark in my soul had been quickly lit igniting hope that there was something *I could do* to help fight this cancer too! Chemotherapy made me feel like death, like I was poisoning myself to get better. It made me sad. What if I could heal my body without poisoning it, but nourishing it? What if I could feel happy and empowered and full of life as I fight the disease in my body? I began to feel excited. A soul raging forest fire of personal research, intrigue, and a movement towards true health in my own life quickly ensued. A stark contrast from the disease management path I had been on. Chemo cuts a tree down to a stump, but it doesn't always get to the root. I wanted to feel good, from the inside out. The feeling of empowerment that I gained was like a cube of ice on a hot, dry tongue. It brought relief.

The message of this documentary promoted the healing power of nutrition over disease. How a plant based, whole foods diet can often keep cancer from developing and spreading inside your body. How creating an alkaline environment keeps disease far away. And not only cancer . . . but many other diseases too, like autoimmune and cardiovascular disease. It explained how green, leafy veggies can create that alkaline environment that cancer cannot thrive in. It described studies that showed how white, refined sugar can act as a fertilizer for cancer, and it is imperative for cancer patients to stay far, far away from it. I learned about the power of antioxidants, and the importance of caring for your gut as it serves as the center of all your immunity. After being mesmerized for the entirety of the documentary I felt like my eyes had just been opened to a whole new world. A world I truly never knew existed. Don't get me wrong, I knew that broccoli was good for you and Dove ice cream bars (one of my personal favorites that my grandma always had well stocked in her freezer) weren't, but I did not understand the significant implications of my food choices. I really didn't.

Our cells are directly affected by the foods we choose to eat. I eat, at minimum, three times a day! I never realized the power I had over my body; I felt like I had a new found authority over my body! Hopeful that I could now make choices with my food that could really help my body fight this disease that was trying to spread inside me. Empowered to make choices with my food that not only would help me get well, but that would allow me to experience health in a life changing, radical, new way.

This news was a gift from God and it opened a world to me that said I was not destined to be a helpless victim caught in cancer's snare. I felt like I had a weapon to help fight this thing. A weapon outside of chemo and radiation that left me feeling sick and tired and poisoned. A hope for health as I had never known it. I had always been intrigued by vegans, and now I was about to become one. I also realized that with this knowledge came great responsibility, like I had to act. This new found knowledge begged me for a response. I had no choice but to at least try it. You don't know what you don't know, but now I knew. I was sick, and I knew of something tangible I could do now to fight to hopefully help myself get better.

"Why doesn't the vast majority of the public know about these things?" I thought to myself. This information truly was life changing for me, and I knew that it would be for other people too . . . *if* they knew about it. It had the potential to be life changing for my peers that sat in the doctor's waiting room anticipating their scheduled "treatment." Each treatment that left them feeling weaker than they did from the time before. There was scientific research, and countless testimonials to back this information up. All I could keep asking was, why haven't we heard about this? I am a nurse! I had been through three years of nursing school and worked full time in the medical field for two years, and I was clueless. When I would walk in to the cancer center and see all those bald heads and eyes full of dread, I wanted so badly to stand on a chair with a megaphone in hand and tell them everything that I was learning so that they too could feel empowered to help themselves try and get healthy again. I became obsessed. One documentary led to another documentary which led to me reading books and articles. I read and watched everything that I could get my hands on. Can too much of a good thing be bad? I was starting to put my heart's hope in my own hands, instead of the Lord . . . never a good idea.

I made fresh pressed juice almost every single morning, sometimes I did it up to two to three times a day. I juiced any and everything that sprang up from the ground. Carrots, ginger, beets, mushrooms, apples, kale, spinach, and cucumber. You name it, I juiced it. I was like a pit bull that was incapable of loosening the grip of his jaws from the rope. I could not let it go. My energy and hope were being poured into a vegan diet, juicing, and coffee enemas. Yes, real caffeinated, organic coffee being gently delivered to your GI tract to cleanse it. And an enema is not delivered to your GI tract via your mouth. I'll leave it there. Don't judge, these little numbers will clean your colon and detoxify your liver like nobody's business. If you have done them, you know exactly what I mean (wink emoji here). In my heart of hearts, I believed these habits were a sure way to get me well and keep me well. I was determined. Have you ever been so locked into an idea that it was all that you could think about? Hashtag obsessed. Yup, that was me. Completely obsessed. Fearful even of a McDonald's cheeseburger, or any other food falling under that umbrella. I felt like one wrong bite and I was feeding the disease inside of my body that I couldn't see. I had no gauge of what was happening inside of me. I was putting a lot of pressure on myself. William could see that it was something I was taking very seriously and he never complained about the abrupt switch our home made to meat free meals. He shoveled in the kale instead of burgers, sweet potatoes instead of chicken, black beans instead of brownies that I began making for our dinners. He ate peanut butter Ezekiel bread sandwiches every day for lunch for nearly three years. For my BBQ, eastern NC raised, meat admiring husband, this act of love meant a lot to me. He truly never once complained, but ate what I prepared with a grateful heart.

I was so intense about these natural healing methods that it became obvious that this is where my hope was coming from. I was trusting nutrition and the healing power I thought that it could bring me above trusting the Lord's good plan for my life. I felt like I had some control, and I liked that. Control is at the root of so much of the sin in my life. I was looking for something my Martha-heart could *do*. And there is nothing wrong with doing. There is nothing wrong with me being a plant-based eater. Doing is really good a lot of times, but my doing was replacing my believing . . . believing that God is the manager of each one of the cells in my body. Control is an illusion that feels so comforting when things feel so out of control. Can I get an amen from the choir?

I planned to share this newly discovered "hope" with any other cancer patient or medical professionals willing to listen. My instinct was to bombard anyone open to listening about alternative forms of treatment (remember me mentioning my desire for the purse sized megaphone?), but I quickly realized that many people were very skeptical of these types of non-traditional approaches. I quickly learned the word "quack" that is common in these conversations. A quack is basically someone who brings a new idea that isn't common in western medicine and involves some form of non-man-made treatment. In my opinion, a quack is often used to describe anything that doesn't involve a FDA approved medication.

I wanted to stop taking chemotherapy so badly. I only had about three or four treatments left when I discovered this wealth of knowledge. I remember sitting in the car with William, in the driveway of our townhome, begging him to be on board with me stopping the chemotherapy treatment. I was half way finished with the four month treatment. He tenderly, but adamantly pleaded with me to continue it. He was open minded, and had become a believer even in the whole foods, plant-based lifestyle, but he was scared too. The concept was still so new to him. So different than what we had seen others do. We were both scared. It was an emotional conversation. There were tears on both sides, as the car engine jolted again having been in park for thirty minutes in the driveway. The sun was setting and the sky was its orange, yellow, pink NC spring setting self. "Catherine, if I lose you, I'll always wonder if stopping the chemo had something to do with it. I'll never forgive myself." "But I'm the one going through the aftershocks of it rocking my system," I explained. We sat silently, hand in hand, tears rolling down our cheeks. Angry, afraid, and discouraged that we were having to even have this conversation. He asked me a bold question, "Will you do it for me, please?" I sat quietly, staring at the floorboard, thinking. After a long pause, "For you, I guess so." I responded. "But, if it doesn't work, or it comes back, I'm not doing chemo again." He agreed. He turned the key ignition to shut the overheating engine off. We walked silently inside and went up to bed.

My last scan had showed that the cancer was receding. I didn't know for sure whether it was going away because of the chemo or from all of the juicing and high doses of raw green leafies I was consuming every day. Regardless of what was working, probably both, my body was responding positively. The cancer was going away. Hopefully into a black hole in outer space never to return.

Even when I felt so strongly about the healing power of nutrition and using that to fight the disease inside my body, I also instinctively knew that every cancer patient's journey with the sickness is very personal. Very individualized. So, I tried not to be pushy about it to other patients, even though I naturally can be a, eh-hem, passionate person. If they weren't interested, I left the topic alone. I would always tell them, "For what it's worth, this is something that has been very powerful in my journey . . . take it or leave it." I would tell them the information and then leave the subject alone, not bringing it up again. I did this when I was "on the clock," and when I was at the hospital as a patient. With doctors, however, including my own, I felt bitter and disillusioned during this time. I know I shouldn't have been that way, but I was. Looking back, I believe now, for the most part, they were just trying to do the best they could with the information they had been given in medical school. I am not bitter anymore now that I am not in the heat of the battle, but I am often saddened that many medical doctors in the United States don't give more thought, investigation, or credit to nutrition as a form of viable medical treatment. Including cancer treatment.

If all doctors believed that nutrition can be a powerful healing tool, they could offer it to the sick people under their care. I asked my oncologist his opinion of the healing power of nutrition, and he said he didn't believe that there was any substantial evidence to back it up. Unfortunately, both the doctors and the patients are not aware that it is viable option (maybe some doctors are aware but choose to continue pushing traditional treatment options because they are so lucrative for the pharmaceutical industry, government and FDA). But I don't think that most doctors, who are in the business of helping others, are that greedy or mean spirited. I certainly don't believe that my oncologist is that greedy. He was a kind man who, I could tell, truly believed in the work that he was doing. I just think they truly don't know. It's not discussed in the training that they receive. In medical school in the United States, students receive very little education on nutrition and an enormous amount of education on pharmaceutical related treatments and symptom management. I was so grateful that my patient shared that information with me that day. It did change my life, just like he had said that it had changed his.

In the meantime, I continued working as a nurse. Because of my suspicion towards the way Western medicine focuses on treating the symptoms rather than the root of sickness or prevention, I thought seriously about quitting, especially as I spent so much time working in the cancer center. I contemplated going to work with my dad in the corporate world, attending massage therapy school, starting a juicing food truck, or going back to school to study to become a naturopathic doctor. But, for whatever reason, I didn't pursue any of those things. I did, however, become keenly aware of the link between food and sickness/health, the FDA and the pharmaceutical industry. I began to better understand how they were all connected. I saw what foods our government chooses to subsidize and make cheap for the public. I quickly learned I would have to use nearly my whole paycheck to cover the expense of organic fruits and vegetables. I was basically already doing that. I knew how I would fix that problem. I would grow my own food! And through trial and error, that is exactly what I did. I didn't realize at the time, but this new hobby would not only be healing for my body, it would be healing for my soul too . . . because more heartache lay ahead. But unlike cancer, which was something in my body that I didn't want there, this heartache involved something I desperately wanted inside my body that wouldn't come . . . a baby.

CHAPTER 7

A New Beginning

"I can discover that our greatest testimony isn't found in those moments of
victory over weakness or even in moments of hope fulfilled. It is found in
waiting, wanting, adoring. It is found in hunger."

—SARA HAGERTY[1]

"Why did we do this to ourselves? I know that we wanted a vegetable
garden, but did our first garden really need to be 1200 square feet?" To a girl
who grew up in the suburbs, I felt like I was living on a small farm. I *loved* it.

That's a lot of space. At the time, I thought that three rows of okra would
be a satisfactory amount. Yep, I'd say that it turned out to be a satisfactory
amount! I didn't realize that one stalk of okra produces many pieces of okra
a day. We ended up growing enough of it for the United States Military.
At this point, though, I had never grown a vegetable a day in my life. My
ambition superseded my logic when we, correction, William, began tilling
our garden space. I kept having him add on to the space. "Just a bit more,"
I would say, "enough for one more row." Thank goodness for YouTube and
Barnes and Noble. In hindsight I am so glad that we created our first garden
to be so big. I may not have felt that way when I was weeding and watering it, but I know that it was the challenging and therapeutic hobby that
I needed at that time. My heart was longing for a child but month after

1. Hagerty. *Every Bitter Thing.* 186

month my body would signal to me that what my heart was wanting did not match what was happening, or not happening, inside of my body.

As I dug in the dirt, I considered the way I had been rolling in the dirt with the Lord. The way Jacob wrestled on the ground with the Lord. I'm sure their wrestling match caused some ground to be broken and some dirt to stick under his fingernails. Some mud on his boots (or maybe sandals?) and some brown smeared on his cheeks.

> "And Jacob was left alone. And a man wrestled with him until the breaking of the day. When the man saw that he did not prevail against Jacob, he touched his hip socket, and Jacob's hip was put out of joint as he wrestled with him. Then he said, "Let me go, for the day has broken." But Jacob said, "I will not let you go unless you bless me." And he said to him, "What is your name?" And he said, "Jacob." Then he said, "Your name shall no longer be called Jacob, but Israel, for you have striven with God and with men, and have prevailed." Then Jacob asked him, "Please tell me your name." But he said, "Why is it that you ask my name?" And there he blessed him. So Jacob called the name of the place Peniel, saying, "For I have seen God face to face, and yet my life has been delivered." The sun rose upon him as he passed Penuel, limping because of his hip." Genesis 32:24-31

I was wrestling with the Lord too. I knew the soil was being turned up from the ground. New growth was bound to be breaking through the earth. The question was, when was I going to witness it?

The fresh produce at the health stores was expensive. I liked the idea of growing our own food. Homesteading has always been something that has interested us. I get a deep satisfaction out of being able to produce, especially when it involves my family's needs being met. I am simple minded and love the idea of being self-sustainable. Although we are far from self-sustainable, the bit we have learned about gardening and cooking from scratch has been fun and rewarding. This garden excited us. It was new and it had a lot to do with us moving out to the country. It represented health. Wellness. Growth. A fresh start in a wide-open area. A new beginning.

To eat a vegetable dinner that evolved from a seed in my hand to a plant bearing fruit in my backyard fills up my soul as much as it does my belly. To run my hands through the black dirt and be alone with the plants and the dog while the sun heats my back is a place of worship for me. As I type this, I close my eyes and can feel the cool breeze brush my face as sweat drips down my dirt covered brow. As I take my hands out of my gardening gloves for a moment to breathe, I feel God's peace engulf me. As I stand to stretch my back after having been bent over picking the long, green, stubborn weeds (that seem to laugh at my efforts to conquer them) I think about the weeds of sin in my heart that I must intentionally root out of my life. As I hear the horse's deep exhalations in the pasture to my right I am reminded of God's magnificence and power. As I watch the tall gumball trees sway in the wind, I feel God's presence. As I admire the butterflies that are drawn in time and time again to the bright, beautiful flowers that match their magnificent wings I see God's beauty. Yes, it's place that screams God's existence, love and presence to me over and over, causing my heart to fall at his feet in surrender.

Do you get satisfaction out of watching something grow? I sure do. To witness growth is a beautiful thing. In fact, it's a sacred thing. We watch our children grow. We watch ourselves grow. We watch our succulents grow in our kitchen windowsills. Growth is right and beautiful. There are so many powerful lessons paralleling life that I have learned through gardening. Humans are a lot like vegetable plants. *We all weather storms, endure pests, and hopefully, by the grace of God, survive and bear fruit.* Plants grow in silence. I consider how our lives are so loud sometimes. So electronic-filled. So busy. So hurried. Thanks to social media, so public. Rushing from one responsibility to the next. I get tired of always rushing. Do you? It is so refreshing to dig in the dirt, to pick a vine ripened tomato, to smell a bright green basil leaf, to taste and savor the sweetness of a fresh piece of corn. To sit on the edge of the garden and admire all the magnificent colors, God's handiwork, and the tangible fruit of your hard labor. Towering green stalks and ready-to-be-picked fruit . . . therein lies a sense of accomplishment and pride.

As a Christian, I see the value of the hippie's perspective on the worth of nature. Nature "knowing best." But really, it is God who knows best. *He created* the nature. The less that we (humans) tamper with it, the better off we will be. *Food, in its natural state, is a strong medicine and it can do a lot of good for our bodies.* This is the belief I have come to. Eating food from my garden felt like eating food straight from the hand of God, and I enjoyed it. I felt like what I was putting into my body was good and right.

The days that my dachshund, Daisy, and I spent out in the garden at our house on Pond Valley Lane were some of my favorite days. We built that house. It had been a fun project and an exciting distraction as I walked out of cancer's dark tunnel. Days in the garden were days filled with lots of solitude. A very real change of pace. Life moves a little bit slower in the country. The horses were grazing in the pasture beside us, the donkeys were being their usual, temperamental selves, deer scurried in the distance, and we were all just doing our own thang. I was working part-time as a nurse, and Daisy and I would go out to the garden and spend hours in it on my days off. I would pick okra, and she would steal it from my harvesting basket. At first it annoyed me, but then I came to laugh at it. I never knew a dog could be so into okra. We ended up munching on raw okra together a lot after I learned how much she liked it. I would throw her the overgrown, tough pieces and she would pounce on them as if she had just discovered gold. Overgrown okra is almost impossible to chew, but those were Daisy's favorite pieces.

My favorite things to grow in the garden that first summer after we moved to the country were okra and sunflowers. Some of the sunflowers were as big as my head. The bumblebees loved them. They almost loved them as much as the butterflies loved the Lantana. We grew cucumbers, tomatoes, watermelons, corn, blackberries, cilantro, squash, peppers, and zinnias. We even planted a fig tree and blueberry bushes. We got tired of eating the squash but never the okra. In fact, I still have several bags of squash in the freezer right now from June, it's March. We ate okra every way you can possibly make it. We boiled, fried, stewed, steamed and baked it. Just like Bubba did with his shrimp in *Forest Gump*. I can taste that okra now as I write this. I can barely wait to get those seeds in the ground again this coming spring, to water and care for them, and eat the *gifts* that come up from that dirt.

The vibrant colors in a garden remind me of the life that it represents. At that time, it was something for me to nurture. I liked cultivating life from these plants. I had recently learned that it was going to be much more difficult for my womb to bear life than I had anticipated. The therapy of these quiet hours in the garden were straight from the hand of God. The time spent inside its gate was soul-healing. God's timing for that season out in the solitude of the country, working a new hobby, was perfect. It would be him ministering to my aching soul . . . surrounding me with his creation.

"For everything there is a season, and a time for every matter under heaven:

a time to be born, and a time to die;

a time to plant, and a time to pluck up what is planted;

a time to kill, and a time to heal;

a time to break down, and a time to build up;

a time to weep, and a time to laugh;

a time to mourn, and a time to dance;

a time to cast away stones, and a time to gather stones together;

a time to embrace, and a time to refrain from embracing;

 a time to seek, and a time to lose;

a time to keep, and a time to cast away;

a time to tear, and a time to sew;

a time to keep silence, and a time to speak;

a time to love, and a time to hate;

a time for war, and a time for peace.

What gain has the worker from his toil? I have seen the business that God has given to the children of man to be busy with. He has made everything beautiful in its time. Also, he has put eternity into man's heart, yet so that he cannot find out what God has done from the beginning to the end. I perceived that there is nothing better for them than to be joyful and to do good as long as they live; also that everyone should eat and drink and take pleasure in all his toil—this is God's gift to man."

—Ecclesiastes 3:1-13

CHAPTER 8

Another Diagnosis

"When you pass through the waters, I will be with you; and through the rivers, they shall not overwhelm you; when you walk through the fire you shall not be burned, and the flame shall not consume you."

—ISAIAH 43:2

There is something deep inside the heart of most women that longs to give and nurture life. Prior to infertility, I thought there was only one way to fulfill that longing, to be a mother. It is why many little girls play with "their babies." I remember when I was a little girl, my favorite game was to play house underneath the grand piano in the garage-turned-playroom at my parent's house. If I played house outside, it was always in my wooden playhouse. I preferred to play the game inside because I was not allowed to take my American Girl doll baby stroller and her wrought-iron bed outside in the sandbox. I had two American Girl dolls, Samantha and Felicity. They, of course, were my two daughters, one adopted and one biological, and I pretended my husband was away at war. The story was always the same. I dressed my "daughters" up in cute outfits, talked to them, brushed their hair, tucked them into bed, pushed them in their strollers and made sure they had everything that they needed to reach their dreams. I loved to make them "mud pies" in the sandbox. I would delicately top the "pie" with berries from the holly bush that stood in the front yard. That would serve as dinner. I loved taking care of my baby doll daughters. I found great satisfaction there. It came naturally. No one had to teach or rehearse with me how to do it. As a five-year-old girl it was instinctive. Natural. Obvious. From the time I was a young child, there has been a God-given instinct for me to give and nurture life. As a child, I never questioned if the basketball that I would put under my shirt (pretending I was pregnant) would never become a reality for me. It was always assumed that it would. *But God had other plans for me.* Some plans that I wanted and some that I did not want. And, *many* that I did not understand.

Infertility weds with it a type of pain that is hard to bear. A pain that cuts deeply and causes the blood to pour out freely. A pain that I had never experienced, even from cancer. This type of pain changes a woman forever. The cancer diagnosis and treatment were difficult, but the infertility diagnosis soon after was a much more severe blow. Emotionally, I felt like I was sinking into a pit that no one could help me get out of. A pit of pain and loss. The loss is real. And forever. The void is overwhelming. The sharpest knife in its block of torture is the loneliness. When the reality of knowing that you will never carry a child in your womb is realized, it is so easy to withdraw into a shell of isolation. This is true for me even now. Isolation is the best friend of darkness. Infertility is married to a very real, deep, profound sense of loss. It's strange and paradoxical the way that the emptiness of infertility is such a heavy weight to bear. The weight of it is carried in your heart instead of your belly. Sleepless nights have nothing to do with the extra weight putting a strain on your lower back or your growing girth pressing on your diaphragm making it hard to breathe, but rather the ache of your heart that is longing for those inconvenient experiences of pregnancy. Researchers have likened the heartache of infertility to the despair of learning that you have a terminal illness. It is a heartache that has the potential to drown you in your own tears. Breathing feels like a chore.

We never expected the news that we got that day in the doctor's office. We had been "trying" for a little over a year. After having waited two and a half years because of my cancer, it felt like it had been longer than a year of trying with no success. We were about to start trying to get pregnant when I learned I had cancer. My treatment took six months and then we were told to wait two more years from when my treatment ended. Many people have trouble getting pregnant initially, I thought to myself. I really didn't think that we were that abnormal. I just never expected to be told that we would not have biological children outside of invasive surgery and in-vitro fertilization when we went in for, what I thought was, a check-off-the-list consultation. A consultation that I had believed, at that time, was nothing more than a formality in this whole investigative process. It took the doctor a sixty second test to give William and I a diagnosis that would break our hearts forever. "You're not getting pregnant because of a congenital defect that affects roughly one to two percent of the male population" he told us. I scooted to the edge of my seat, and leaned in closer turning my ear towards him to make sure I just heard him correctly. "What?" I said. William's head dropped and his eyes looked down at the floor as he shook his head and rubbed his eyes. The look on his face was so full of despair that I will never be able to erase the look in his eyes in that moment for as long as I live. "I'm sorry." He immediately said. We hugged. I began to cry, a skill I had become a professional at.

Dumbfounded. That is probably the best way to describe our reaction that afternoon. I felt like I had just been hit in the face with a frying pan. Sitting in the doctor's office, it felt like my heart sank into my abdomen. It became hard to swallow because of the lump in my throat. I felt so sad for William. I knew this diagnosis would rock his feeling of manhood in a way that I would never be able to fully understand. This man who wanted to give me the world, I could already see the self-induced guilt in his eyes that he couldn't give me a biological child. I couldn't believe what the doctor was telling us. It felt surreal. "No, please," I wanted to say to him, "take it back. You don't mean that. Not for us." It reminds me now of when God called Moses to lead the Jewish people out of slavery in Egypt. "But Moses said to the Lord, 'Oh my Lord, I am not eloquent, either in the past or since you have spoken to your servant, but I am slow of speech and of tongue.' Then the Lord said to him, 'Who has made man's mouth? Who makes him mute, or deaf, or seeing, or blind? Is it not I, the Lord? Now therefore go, and I will be with your mouth and teach you what you shall speak. But he said, 'Oh, my Lord, please send someone else.'" Exodus 4:10-13. That is what I wanted to say to the Lord that day and the days following. "Oh Lord, you don't want to choose *us* to carry this load. Oh Lord, please, please choose someone else. Not us, Lord. Please, don't let this call . . . this withholding . . . fall on us."

After the heart wrenching news was delivered, William and I were quickly and confidently reassured that a remedy could be pursued in a laboratory setting. I barely heard the words of the doctor as we both sat stunned from this left-field ambush attack on our hearts. The tissue I was holding in my hand was quickly drenched with my tears that I was trying to hold back but couldn't. I reached and decided to grab the whole box; one tissue wouldn't do for this. A surgery could be performed and the needed elements could be retrieved from our bodies to create life . . . beginning in a petri dish, the doctor explained to us. I tried to listen and receive the information that the doctor reassured us with, but the pit in my stomach, the nausea, and tears were begging for my attention. "Can we have a minute?" I asked the doctor. He nodded and stepped out, closing the door behind him.

I don't pass any judgement on people or friends who choose the fertility assistance route. I know many who have. However, at least then, and for now, it is not the route for us. The journey of infertility is a highly sensitive and personal road. We are big believers in natural and holistic approaches to medicine. In-vitro fertilization just wasn't something that either of us had peace about pursuing at the time. We thought seriously about it, but it didn't take long for us to have an open conversation about it with each other. Only a few days after this doctor's visit, and having already pursued fertility medications, scans, blood tests, different positions, ovulation charting, timed sex, we were spent. We were tired of feeling like lab rats. Like robots. We were tired of "timing" our romance. Our relationship. Our love. It had taken its toll on us individually and as a couple. It can wear a love story down and then kick you while you are down. It is easy to get lost in your goal as couple . . . to conceive a child. It's easy to lose sight of the love that you used to share in that place. Intimacy turns into a meeting. One that is on a very strict timeframe, with no room for deviation or spontaneity or passion. The emotional toll it takes on you can easily leave your marriage hanging by a thread. Hanging on only by a commitment you made before the Lord.

I had eaten avocados out the wazoo because I had read about how the folic acid in them helps you get pregnant. We had both been eating right, exercising, praying faithfully . . . doing everything in our power to get pregnant. But the truth is, if you do everything the doctors, friends, pregnancy magazines and online articles tell you to do, you still can't make yourself get pregnant. You can do yoga headstands all day long while inhaling guacamole down the hatchet and laying still and flat as a eastern North Carolina roadkill on a hot, summer day after timed sex, but still, *nothing is going to get you pregnant unless God himself intervenes.* Desperate times call for desperate measures though . . . .and we had tried it all. All within our power. All within the context of our home and not a medical facility.

We chose together very soon after we learned the news, "If God wants us to have a biological child, then he will work a miracle inside of our bodies." And we trusted that he would do it as a display of his power . . . His majestic work of art. Not because it is a gift that we demand to be given by him. Not because it is something that we manipulate on a scientific level to make happen for ourselves (although that would be his creation too). But because he chooses it for us, in the context that we have peace about. We both have full confidence that he is capable of causing us to conceive. It is something that we continue to ask him for. It's something that we continue to believe he can do. I don't care what the doctor said. The plans of the Lord cannot be thwarted. If he chooses not to do this, we accept that, with broken and faith filled hearts.

Psalm one hundred and seven is a place my heart parks for comfort. The power of God described in these verses causes me to close my eyes and breathe a deep sigh of relief. The pressure is not on me to get what I want. The Lord gives and takes away according to his will, and his power makes him *unstoppable*. This really does put my heart at ease. Verse twenty-five says, "For he commanded and raised the stormy wind, which lifted up the waves of the sea." Verses 28-29 read, "Then they cried to the Lord in their trouble, and he delivered them from their distress. He made the storm be still, and the waves of the sea were hushed." I figured that *if I believe that God can raise and calm the waves of the ocean, he can do whatever he wants in the bodies of myself and my husband. He has no limits. He has no boundaries. All of nature, including our bodies, must answer to his commands.*

The real question is, do I believe he speaks over my life according to his will, or is this all just happenstance? Is this coincidence, or do I have a loving Father that sees me? What about you? What about your pain? Your brokenness? Your spouse's brokenness? Is it chance or *is he doing something?* We went to the doctor's office that day, expecting to go back to work after our appointment. But, with this news, and our hearts feeling stunned, we wisely decided to head home instead. The news had caught us so off-guard. We had thought this appointment was going to pan out to be nothing. We assumed the fertility struggles were related to my cancer treatment. But no. It was a completely separate, unrelated battle. Going back into work and pretending like everything was "normal" was just not something either of us were capable of doing. We could not put on a fake professional game face. Our hearts were broken and it showed on our faces and through our many tears. We both knew that this forty-five-minute doctor's visit had just changed our lives forever. The following days would bring incomprehensible despair. Our tears could not be controlled, held back, or minimized. I begged God to, "hear my cry, O God, listen to my prayer; from the end of the earth I call to you when my heart is faint, lead me to the rock that is higher than I." Psalm 61:1-2. He was my rock. But after a few days of processing, I got angry. And you better believe I intended to let him know it. One of many reasons for this anger was that this doctor's visit was on the anniversary of my finishing cancer treatment two years prior. Thus, the date we were told we couldn't have biological children by the doctor was the same date we had been given the green light from the cancer doctor to try. I was so hurt by this, what felt like, horribly mean timing.

I sat on our large front porch, staring out at the horses grazing in the pasture beside our small country home. This spot would be my infirmary for months to come. My sanctuary of grief. On that porch swing, I spent hours crying out to God from the pit of my soul. When I think about infertility, my mind goes to that spot, on that front porch, at that house. I would watch the horses and think to myself, what is their purpose? Do they ever get bored eating grass all day? The tone of my heart was bitter and mocking as I questioned this scene in front of me. Do they ever get bitter at the gnats constantly nagging them? What are they thinking? I know what I am thinking. I am hurting. Deep pain that makes it hard to even stand up. Pain that makes it hard to get out of bed. Pain that leaves me feeling numb to the world. Pain that makes me want to see and speak to no one. My positivity had been traded for pessimism. And I felt it. I was aching. The constant lump in my throat and chest felt like a weight that I was shackled to. I wanted the key to detach myself from it, but I was too emotionally exhausted to even think where to begin looking for that key. Even if I found the key, I thought to myself, this feeling will never go away.

It's a pain that transcends cultures and time. Women from generations past, and women on the other side of the world, regardless of race, language, cultural differences, socioeconomic differences, all have a deep understanding of one another's loss. Many of us experience infertility for a thousand different reasons. But the reason doesn't matter, there is a unity among us that transcends our differences. "Those horses will never know this level of pain," I thought to myself as I continued to watch them graze. Their life is so simple, so peaceful. Our neighbor's eighteen horses that grazed in the field to the right of our house were such a strange comfort to me. Like an old, understanding friend. A friend that I didn't feel like I had.

At this point most of my friends already had one, two, some even three little ones. I didn't have to explain my thoughts or numb emotions to the horses, they were just present with me. We had no connection to one another, but, for whatever reason, they soothed the sting of my pain, at least a little bit. And I would sit and watch them for many days to come.

CHAPTER 9

What Infertility Taught me About Relationships

"Jesus has shown us how to love: Look, feel, and then help. If we help someone but don't take the time to look at the person and feel what he or she is feeling, our love is cold. And if we look and feel, but don't do what we can to help, our love is cheap. Love does both."

—PAUL MILLER[1]

Women who have never experienced infertility cannot understand the profound sense of loss that is the constant companion of this diagnosis. How can they? How can any of us truly understand a road we have never walked? Shared experiences are a powerful unifier, but they are also not the only column that supports true friendship. When someone you love is hurting, you hurt too. And the friend that you are hurting for, knows and feels your pain. That kind of friendship offers comfort and love in a very special way. That kind of loyalty glues you to another soul in a life altering, "I'll never forget your kindness to me" type of way. I know, because of God's grace, I have experienced those types of friendships in some of my darkest hours.

Her name is Myrlande. She is loyal to a fault. It's one of the things I love most about her. Although I've never tried to record a list of her good

---

1. Miller. *Love Walked.* 28.

traits; the task would be far too overwhelming. To meet a mother that can regularly discuss topics outside of motherhood with genuine interest is a rare and beautiful thing. And my friend, Myrlande, mother of three, is really good at that. She regularly plans dates with me without bringing her children. She will never know how much this has meant to me over the past years. I enjoy my friend's kids, but to all the mother wannabes out there walking through the fire of infertility . . . *to have a girlfriend that pursues your friendship outside of the world of her children is the greatest gift an infertile woman can be given.* It's a way to wink at her and say, I care about you, friend. Oh, the depth of how much this means to an infertile woman. My heart will always be truly touched by her initiative and thoughtfulness. In fact, as I write this, she is coming over tomorrow to go for a walk, eat lunch, and go consignment shopping. She is not doing this because she has the extra time . . . she is a wife, a mother of three children, a foster parent, and a leader to her daughter's Girl Scout troop. Her mother lives with her, and she holds a job. She is busy. What a treasure her free time is. I am consistently humbled that she chooses to spend any of it with me. But she doesn't view it like that. She just serves with a joyful heart. This friend is one of my heroes.

I pray to be that kind of friend. To learn from Myrlande's example of friendship to me. God's truths transcend our inability to fully empathize and can speak into the loneliest, most destitute soul. "So now faith, hope, and love abide, these three; but the greatest of these is love." 1 Corinthians 13:13. This love makes it easier to "bear one another's burdens, and so fulfill the law of Christ." Galatians 6:2. My point is, Myrlande has never been infertile. But that doesn't entirely matter. The love of Christ flows through her so much that it transcends our different life experiences.

Myrlande wasn't the only friend that was a mother and a gift to me during that time. There were others. A thoughtful gift from the Lord that I don't receive lightly. At the time I was deeply grieving the loss of ever having biological children, my sister, Elizabeth, and my precious friend Jennifer, in particular, loved on me with beautiful empathy and tender kindness during my darkest night. Their love touched me, because I felt it, even when their life was full of so much tangible "motherhood." They taught me so much, and they had no idea they were teaching. They were just living, and by doing that they were being flickers of light in my darkness. Like Myrlande, life did not call them to endure this road, but that didn't matter in the love they offered to me. They cared for me and were a source of comfort to me regardless. They listened, cried with me, prayed over me, consistently reached out to me as I retreated and I knew they bore my burden in their own hearts. They were kind to me when I wasn't always very loveable . . . or likeable. I remember Jennifer sitting on the red, yellow, and green checkered chair in my living room, as I sat of the floor, legs crossed like a pretzel. I was telling her how much I was struggling. She didn't say anything. She just listened . . . .and then she began to cry. I've never felt so loved, as I did in that moment. She grieved beside me, and I just watched her. The dimly lit floor lamp behind the chair she was sitting in lit her face and illuminated the tears I saw streaming down her cheeks. I was so moved. My sister, who at the time lived in another city, would call weekly to check on me and make visits (with two toddlers in tow) out into the country to see me. She found out she was unexpectantly pregnant with her third daughter during this time. She wrote me the kindest, most endearing letter, sent by mail. I read it, and remember feeling so touched that she would "break the news" to me in such a tender way. She ended her two page, hand written letter with, don't call me or talk to me until you are ready. I will not be hurt. I understand this must be so difficult for you. Even she didn't understand why God was gifting her again and not giving me what we were both asking him to. Just to hear her reassure me, gave me the permission to cry and not feel guilty about it. A gift she will likely never know how much it meant. I am crying now as I type and remember this moment.

These precious friends truly cared. They truly hated this too. That meant a lot because I felt so alone. Them hating this with me made me feel not as alone. They taught me what sensitivity looks like. I took mental notes and put them in my back pocket, hoping to later implement the things they (unknowingly) were teaching me. I noticed their thoughtfulness and was impressed by their kindness, even when they had no idea what this felt like personally. It touched me more than tongue can tell. They taught me how to be a good listener. They taught me that it's better to ask the hard questions instead of ignoring the obvious because the conversation could get uncomfortable. They taught me not to shy away from the tears. They taught me the power of presence. They taught me humility. They taught me the comfort found in an out loud prayer over a friend. *Even if I don't know what they are going through, I try to remember and be this type of friend now.*

My other *very* closest companions as I sat under the rain cloud of infertility were women who had gone through it themselves. They knew the look I had in my eyes. A deep, "I've been there" type of knowing. A type of knowing that came by only one route. Experience. These women that I could meet with, both in-person friends and in the pages of a book (author friends), were the water my dried-sponge-of-a-soul needed. God knew that . . . and provided. They had a way of softening my hardened heart like nothing or no one else could. When I would get bitter, one of them would call by phone or speak to me through the pages of her book. To be around them gave me *companionship and hope*, two of the things that an infertility diagnosis most easily steals from a woman. Loneliness and a feeling of destitution are infertility's closest allies. Seeing these women who had risen above those all too familiar emotions inspired me. This is a big reason I decided to write this book. So dear friend, if you are going thru this hellacious experience, hold on to this one thing that may ease the sting ever so slightly, you have the power to bless another woman who will soon surely follow you. You can bless her with a gift (thankfully) many other women don't have to offer . . . empathy. Raw and unadulterated empathy. As you well know, it is a gift to be able to give that to a woman mourning her forever empty womb.

There were two older women, Abigail and Macon, whose experiences and wisdom were a tremendous help to my aching soul. They each shared their stories with me. Stories that I won't share here. It's theirs to share. But I will share that they have each walked through this fire and they have come out on the other side alive, beautifully intact, and deeply in love with Jesus. Seeing that kind of flourishing amidst a war-torn soul was exactly what I needed. Joyful. I needed to see someone who had survived. Hope filled. And, not only surviving, but thriving and serving Jesus with all of their hearts. *Pouring all their soul into giving life to the people within their reach, though their wombs were empty.*

I was comforted even more deeply by two authors, Sara Hagerty and Heather Avis, who wrote about their similar experiences with infertility. *Every Bitter Thing is Sweet* and *The Lucky Few* are beautifully written books from each of these precious women. I read their stories and it would spark a deep connection between myself and these vulnerable authors whom I had never met. I would feel an intense compassion for their pain. I felt like I had a friend. They are my inspiration for writing this book. *Meeting with these women in their autobiographies was breath to my lifeless soul.* I have written and told them each that. They were my desert oasis in the unforgiving drought. When I was engaged in the pages of these books, I didn't feel so alone. I felt *deeply* understood. I felt safe. I felt like I didn't have to navigate the cobwebs of emotions and try to find the right words to express them.

They had done that for me on the pages of their books. I could just read and relate and breathe, all while sipping a hot mug of coffee and enjoying the softness of my fuzzy socks as my feet rested on my favorite living room chair. The big-armed chair that engulfed me, much like Sara and Heather were doing to my heart in the pages of their writings, offered a reprieve as I turned to the next page entrenched in their words.

Sara Hagerty (who I quote many times throughout this book), in particular, challenged me to crawl into the arms of Jesus and be held by him for as long as I needed. I could easily receive that advice from her because I knew she knew the pain. She had been there. And she knew what Jesus did for her. I was interested in seeing if Jesus could be that kind of comfort to me too. These women, these pen-to-page friends, who could not bear life in their own bodies, gave me life, air, and hope in my sorrow. These women met me in my isolation. *They mothered me.* They took me under their wing and nurtured my aching soul. In the armpit of my life, they cared for me. But really, it was God himself meeting me there. It was God who was mothering me. He sent these angels to minister to his hurting daughter.

I have learned that the Lord doesn't usually concern himself with what we are used to in our relationship with him. He doesn't concern himself with what we are comfortable with. Or even what makes us happy. He asks, how can I get my daughter to love me more deeply, *because I love her.* He loves you too, dear one. Maybe the trial you are walking through right now is the only way for your relationship with him to go to the next level. Is it worth it? If we are being real, some days the answer may be yes! Hallelujah for those faith-filled days! Other days the answer may be no! Like a resounding no. A, let me make sure you hear me loud and clear God, no, no, no! But its ok on those "no" days too. God, the sovereign, relationship treasuring, lover of your soul, his answer . . . His answer is always *yes*! It's totally worth it.

This is what suffering does. Doesn't it? Suffering deepens relationships, both earthly and heavenly ones. I am thankful for the suffering the Lord has called me to thus far in my thirty years. I wouldn't trade it. I really wouldn't. I am not saying that I want the heartache back. I am not hopeful for pain. But I do now see its value. It is easier to acknowledge it when you are on the other side of the pain. I do treasure the things I have learned through the suffering he has called me to, especially the way he has taught me about himself. *Having an eternal perspective eases the sting and bleakness of the miles of desert laying in front of you. In heaven, it'll have been worth it*. In heaven, we can lay in his arms, and know that our suffering on earth allowed us to long for that moment we are (finally) enjoying in his arms, in a way that nothing else could have.

CHAPTER 10

Left Behind

"And when there's nothing left, and we feel we're all in pieces, God begins to make us whole. He makes us real. His love sets us free and transforms us."

—KATIE DAVIS[1]

Baby Showers, please just shoot me. If I am dead, I won't have to make up an excuse as to why I can't come. It's not that I didn't love my friends, but the loneliness I felt in those settings . . . ugh, I am not even sure what to say about it. Terrible is the first word that comes to mind. I felt so much isolation and awkwardness as smiling faces discussed pregnancy and motherhood with so much laughter, joy and anticipation. It can feel like salt in a cut; it burns. It burns enough to get your attention. To make you thrash even, just not outwardly.

I remember one baby shower experience that was especially difficult. It was a shower for a friend that was hosted at one of my best friend's home. I impulsively decided to go. This was soon after our doctor's visit, and it really would have been wisest for me to decline. Regardless, I had RSVP'd "yes" weeks earlier and the day of the shower, I went without giving it the proper amount of forethought, which is a happy-go-lucky personality trait of mine that doesn't always serve me well. I should have paused my busy mind, thought through the situation and given myself permission to choose not to go, but I didn't. The second my foot crossed the threshold of the front

1. Davis. *Kisses from Katie*. 86.

door, I regretted my decision. "Oh, Catherine," I regretfully thought to myself. Why am I here? It was too late at that point. Smiling, warm faces saw me and were welcoming me into the group. Their hospitality and kindness were genuine and generous, but my heart had already begun bleeding out behind the curtain of my forced smile. Just the sight of the blue streamers and adorable baby decorations made my chest and throat throb. I tried my best to offer grins and participate in casual conversations, but I was really struggling to cover up the ache I felt in my chest as I peered across the room at all the "welcome baby" gift bags and saw the freshly-iced, light blue cupcakes on the nearby dining room table. I knew I should not have come, I kept thinking to myself. I didn't want to take away the joy of the mother-to-be by breaking out in tears in front of the group, not to mention their pity. Talk about making a gathering awkward. I just couldn't participate in the celebration that day, but I forced myself to stay a little bit longer. Leaving after having been there only ten minutes would have been far too obvious. I was so angry with myself for not thinking through this more. I was so thankful no one in that room could see the mental battle waging in my head. I should have considered my emotional state that day and wisely declined the invitation. Who cares about an RSVP? Things come up . . . including days of grief and heartache that call for self-care at home. Bubble baths, Bible reading, horse gazing, prayer/fighting with the Lord, toe nail painting, eating vegan treats, book reading these are the quiet, solitary activities it would have been wiser for me to fill this grieving Saturday with. But I chose a baby shower. "Oh Catherine, when will you learn," I thought to myself.

After food and gifts, the group circled up to tell their various labor and delivery experiences. They discussed how long the contractions lasted, whether they birthed naturally or had an epidural, their husband's responses to the contractions, c-section recovery times, breastfeeding troubles and successes, what was working for keeping their toddlers busy, preschool, and on and on. It was hellacious torture for me. I could feel the palms of my hands beginning to sweat and the lump in my throat rising higher and higher. I thought that my chest might crack open in front of everyone and blood come gushing out onto the freshly cleaned hardwood floors. I had to get out of that room. Inside, I could feel myself shrinking, and I thought I might implode. The way that the chairs had been circled up in the living room, and the fact that it was a small gathering with only ten(ish) women there made a premature exit super obvious. I was trying to come up with reasons in my head to get out . . . and fast. It was all I could do to maintain my composure long enough to give a friendly hug and make a quiet beeline exit straight out the door to my car. I told the hostess and mother-to-be that I had somewhere else to be. That "somewhere else" was anywhere else other than that house. I could not be in that room for one more second or I was going to lose it.

Thankfully, I made it to my car and lost it there, away from the group. I felt so alone, which was the most difficult part. Psalm 25:16-21 says, "Turn to me and be gracious to me, for I am lonely and afflicted. The troubles of my heart are enlarged; bring me out of my distress, consider my affliction and my trouble, and forgive all my sins . . . Oh guard my soul and deliver me! Let me not be put to shame, for I take refuge in you. May integrity and uprightness preserve me, for I wait for you." This is how I felt. My sorrow and loneliness drove me deep into the arms of Jesus. And as my dear author friend Sara encouraged, I decided to sit in the arms of Jesus. To let him hold me while I cried it out. With blood pouring out from my pierced heart, I knew he understood. I may not have had a due date or a growing belly, but a new birth was taking place in my soul, I just didn't realize it yet.

The sting that looms in the air of baby showers has lessened significantly with time, although the scab can occasionally fall off and the wound can gush blood even now. The triggers are unpredictable. I still sometimes decline baby shower invitations. It honestly just depends on how close I am to the mother-to-be and how strong I feel on the day of the shower. What is it about time that can be such a profound healer? Maybe it's a combination of distance from the initial blow and perspective. Hopefully it is faith. A faith that has walked through fire and come out on the other side stronger, more resilient, and carrying in my ergo a deeper love for Jesus.

Because of the bond of motherhood, there have been times that I wished that I was a man. I am not suggesting that men don't experience pain with infertility. I know from watching William that their pain is equally real and deep. I am, however, suggesting that the loneliness that accompanies this suffering is not as severe for most men. "Why?" I've pondered. Most men are good at having lives outside of their children. *I see this as a strength.* I have noticed that men are often good at developing their hobbies as adults. They talk about things that don't consistently center around their children, like backpacking adventures, personal goals, and college basketball games. Women, on the other hand, mainly talk about their kids. They talk about their kids a lot. When a woman's full-time job/responsibility is motherhood, it makes sense that this is the most natural topic for her. It makes sense that her day is centered around her kid's schedule. I don't blame her. But I couldn't relate.

Men also don't carry the new life in their wombs. Their body is not involved in the same way a woman's is in the process. A woman's body miraculously houses, nourishes, and grows a little life inside of her own womb. It is astounding. It's beautiful the way she can nourish an infant from her own breast. The physical connection between a mother and child is a miracle. Each and every time. It testifies to the Creator who formed this intimate relationship. During this season of my life, I often felt like I had nothing to contribute to the female conversations, especially in a group setting. I sit on the sideline wanting to be a part, wanting to participate, but powerless to make myself a member of the club.

1 Samuel 1:1-11 speaks of the weeping and worship of Hannah, a barren woman in the Old Testament. A woman that longs to carry life in her womb. What a comfort it was to me that God chose to include this in his Word. It's clear that God knows that a large part of a woman's heart is to bear life in her womb. We see the deep pain of infertility represented in God's Word. And, I see the Lord's compassion towards infertile women by including it in there. It says:

> "There was a certain man of Ramathaim-zophim of the hill country of Ephraim whose name was Elkanah the son of Jeroham, son of Elihu, son of Tohu, son of Zuph, an Ephrathite. He had two wives. The name of the one was Hannah, and the name of the other, Peninnah. And Peninnah had children, but Hannah had no children.
>
> "Now this man used to go up year by year from his city to worship and to sacrifice to the Lord of hosts at Shiloh, where the two sons of Eli, Hophni and Phinehas, were priests of the Lord. On the day when Elkanah sacrificed, he would give portions to Peninnah his wife and to all her sons and daughters. But to Hannah he gave a double portion, because he loved her, though the Lord had closed her womb. And her rival used to provoke her grievously to irritate her, because the Lord had closed her womb. So it went on year by year. As often as she went up to the house of the Lord, she used to provoke her. Therefore Hannah wept and would not eat. And Elkanah, her husband, said to her, 'Hannah, why do you weep? And why do you not eat? And why is your heart sad? Am I not more to you than ten sons?'

"After they had eaten and drunk in Shiloh, Hannah rose. Now Eli the priest was sitting on the seat beside the doorpost of the temple of the Lord. She was deeply distressed and prayed to the Lord and wept bitterly. And she vowed a vow and said, 'O Lord of hosts, if you will indeed look on the affliction of your servant and remember me and not forget your servant, but will give to your servant a son, then I will give him to the Lord all the days of his life, and no razor shall touch his head.'"

I know that just as God had not forgotten his daughter Hannah, he had not forgotten me either. He was, "putting my tears in his bottle" Psalm 56:8. He knows the same about you, dear one. *He is counting your tears.* Collecting them in a bottle. One by one. You are not alone. Whether you feel alone because you are infertile or your spouse is infertile or you have cancer or you or walking through a situation you feel like no one else understands . . . *you are not alone.* God is with you, and he "will never leave you nor forsake you." Hebrews 13:5

CHAPTER 11

Silence

"He always turns, dear one. He looks into our eyes and says, 'Take heart. I am with you. I am for you.' his hem is wide. And whatever we are facing, he is enough. All we have to do is reach for him."

—KATIE DAVIS MAJORS[1]

Silence.

Does Jesus care about the hard days we endure on Earth? Or does he just want us to smile at church and endure the hard stuff with a cheerful heart like a good Christian should? Does he just want me to tell others about him and as long as I do that then we can pass his "faithfulness" test? Have you ever asked these questions? I certainly have. More than once. I have wanted to know. Is he there? Does he hear me? Am I just praying to the ceiling? Why can't I make sense of my life? These are pressing questions that would help me so much *if I could just understand what it is that he is doing*. Because from the outside looking in, it makes no sense. These were the thoughts running through my head as I waited on the Lord to make sense on my heartache. Do you ever feel like you pray only to get silence in return? Does it make you mad? Frustrated? Hurt? There are so many emotions that can overwhelm a broken heart as you try to process circumstances with your sovereign, heavenly Father. Our relationship with

1. Majors. *Daring to Hope*. 117.

the Lord can have its ups and downs, just like any other. Thankfully, the downs, the grudges, the insecurity, the questions, the pouting, the discouraged heart is experienced by only *one* of us in this divine relationship.

I pray, but I only get silence in response. Deafening silence. Silence that some days made my heart boil over with lava-hot anger, leaving me emotionally drained and physically exhausted. I felt like my soul had been abandoned by him in the dark of night. I was spiritually lonely. Hungry for God, but angry at the same time. Does Jesus see us hurting? If he does, does he care? Why won't he intervene on my behalf? Why doesn't he help make this pain go away?

Feelings can be so overwhelmingly strong sometimes, can't they? When your heart is breaking, it is easy to feel betrayed by God. The heartbreak is only magnified when your longing is something that is affirmed in his Word. God often talks about the blessings of fertility as being a gift to his beloved children. To his children that live obediently, children are a reward from the Lord. And I had already been through a cancer battle. Was that not enough? Hadn't I paid my suffering dues? At least for a little while? Why did my husband have to be told that his genes were preventing us from conceiving a child? My heart was angrily screaming, "Really God? A little harsh don't you think?" Does he think I would be an unfit mother? What's the deal, God?

Psalm 127:3 says, "Behold, children are a heritage from the Lord, the fruit of the womb a reward." I had tried to live obediently to the Lord, I thought to myself. I always longed to "do so many things for him." I knew that he didn't need me, but I wanted to live a faithful life unto the Lord. I had made a quote from Elisabeth Elliot my life theme: "I have but one desire now, to live a life of reckless abandon to the Lord, putting all my energy and strength into it."[2] I have loved him, and I desired to live "all in" for him. Now I was left feeling brokenhearted. Shattered. And seemingly alone. "How can I live passionately for you, when I feel abandoned, ignored and hurt by you?" I thought to myself. My trust in him felt broken, my faith was shaken. I knew that the Lord could prevent these bad things from happening to me. And if he could, why wasn't he doing that? I thought he was my good Father and I was his beloved daughter. Then, what the heck was happening?

When I was broken (what felt like beyond repair), I got angry. Psalm 86:1 says, "incline your ear, O Lord, and answer me, for I am poor and

2. Elliot. *Through Gates of Splendor.* 50-51.

needy." A prayer of David that I could relate to. A prayer I sometimes yelled at the Lord. I spent a lot of time in the Psalms during this season of silence. David, the author of many of the Psalms, talked honestly with the Lord when he was hurting. He depended on God when he was desperate. I wanted to depend on God, but I was too busy arguing with him. I was fixating on how hurt I felt by him. My heart felt hard.

My struggle with the Lord during this season reminds me of the stories you hear of children from hard places who thrash at the love of an adopted parent or loving caregiver. They do all they can to keep the longing parent at a distance. They are afraid of being loved because they have been so painfully burned in the past. The advice from professional social workers and child psychologists is to love a child through these rejections, even at your own expense. If the child thrashes and self mutilates, hug the child tighter. Love the child deeper. Hold on to her and *don't let her go.* Many times, you see the child eventually collapse in the arms of the patient, committed parent. Sometimes out of a surrender of the will, sometimes out of exhaustion. It can be a moment of great triumph in the relationship. God held me, his thrashing, angry daughter, tight and close. *He didn't let me go.*

With the cancer, as the weeks wore on and the treatment continued, I would lose a little bit more of my strength, hair, and positivity with each week. I would come to learn that *God did care.* Later, throughout the heat of infertility, as friend's baby pictures turned into toddler pictures, which turned into school age pictures, and I was spending another holiday season and family beach vacation childless, I came to learn that *God did care.* As my heart longed to adopt and God would not give me the green light, I realized God saw my heart . . . and *God did care.* I can honestly say there wasn't a specific moment, event or conversation when I realized this. It happened though, and it happened over time. The more I, sometimes even sheepishly, walked into the front bedroom, a room I had been saving to be the nursery for my biological and adopted children, yet continued, year after year, to remain empty with William's ugly guitar chords strung across the floor, and sat quietly on the floor with my tears and God's Word open before me— this—this is where these realizations that God cared began becoming more real to me. My desperation was growing as my womb and childless arms were remaining empty.

What are you wondering if God cares about that is weighing heavy on your heart? Let me assure you, dear one, *God cares* about your heart too. Rest assured; he cares. But this isn't anything that someone else can convince you of. You'll have to experience it for yourself. And if you are in a place of utter despair, I'll believe it for you, even if you can't right now.

Better than just caring, *he was with me* in the darkness. He gently opened the door to my heart as I was slamming drawers and doubting him with what felt like an endless flow of tears running from my eyes. *He saw me at the loneliest and lowest point of my life and he entered my pain with me.* He came over and tenderly took me in his arms and held me as I cried. A wedge was silently forming between William and I as I fought to not resent his not consenting to my desire for adoption and as he fought to not resent my pushiness on the subject. The darkness continued but I knew God was in it too.

Nothing around me changed, but something inside of me began to change. He was softening me. Because I recognized that I was beginning to really believe that he was with me in this pain, it couldn't consume me, like I had once wondered if it would. I wasn't by myself. *You are not by yourself either.* God enters our pain with us. And *he will stay with you until the storm is passed and the suns rays are warming your face again.* Who can we "be with" in their pain? That's what Jesus did for me. It was powerful. More powerful than words telling me why I should have faith, or why I should not feel a certain way, or why I should "look on the bright side of things." Jesus didn't tell me any of those things. He was simply with me. And it was his presence that changed things for me. As his hands and feet on Earth, maybe we would do well to "be" with loved ones in their pain, rather than preach at others in their pain. May our hope be that Jesus' loving, "for them" presence in their darkest hour will cause their heart to look heavenward as a flower lifts its face to the sun's bright, beaming rays. That's what my dear friend, Jennifer, did for me. She came to me, sat with me, walked quietly with me in the woods behind our home. Was it Jennifer, or was it Jesus? Or both . . . ?

The weight of the pain of potentially never being granted motherhood (to biological or adopted children) was more than I could bear, and he knew that. My heart ached for both so badly that it felt like it couldn't go on beating. So, out of exhaustion, I collapsed in his lap and spent another afternoon on the floor crying in the empty nursery while William was at work and Daisy sat by the window savoring the many scents of the country. God saw how much my heart longed for motherhood. He felt the pain in my teeth and gums from the chemo. I am not really sure how or when I came to this realization. But I am okay with that. It happened over a period of time.

It's still happening. *What matters is that I knew that he was sitting with me in the dark.* Something inside my soul just believed that he cared. That he saw my pain. That he was with me. I felt his presence. And I felt peace in the darkness. I stopped thrashing and began accepting and believing. Believing that he was the loving and good Father that he said he was. And trusting, though no green light with adoption, though unable to conceive, though unsure if the cancer would ever return I was still his beloved daughter. Are you in a dark place? *God sees you. God loves you. God cares about your pain. He wants to hold you through it. He wants to love you through it. Will you melt into his arms and let him nurture you as you grieve? And if you can't melt in his arms, then just sit there, even if it's begrudgingly, and see if his gentle ways woo you in a little closer.*

It is ok to feel down when things are hard. I have come to learn that guilt-tripping yourself into feeling how you think you *ought to feel* (is there such a thing?) or *how others want or think you should feel* is not necessary . . . or helpful. God can meet you *exactly* where you are. I used to hate the thought of disappointing the people I love when I was feeling down. I am a people pleaser by nature. Even if that meant faking "ok" when I wasn't. Cancer, infertility, and an unfulfilled longing for adoption taught me that God is not threatened by my discouragement. In fact, *my weakness was a launching pad for real intimacy with him.*

"Likewise the Spirit helps us in our weakness. For we do not know what to pray for as we ought, but the Spirit himself intercedes for us with groaning's too deep for words. And he who searches hearts knows what is the mind of the Spirit, because the Spirit intercedes for the saints according to the will of God." Romans 8:26-27.

I spent a lot of time (and still do some days) sitting at his feet, in the quiet, with my discouraged heart spread out before him. I listen to him whisper to me, "my grace is sufficient for you, for my power is made perfect in weakness" 2 Corinthians 12:9. He is big enough to handle my hurts and my doubts. I have come to realize how important authenticity really is. We don't have to fear it. Without it, there will be no real growth for any of us. No real connection with God and with others. If you are afraid of being authentic because people might not like you or admire you, not to worry. You are adored, accepted, and treasured by God. I mainly learned this from David in the Psalms. David kept things real. Pouring his heart out over and over before the Lord, and ending each time with his hope in God. His rawness is an inspiration. As is his confidence that the Lord was able to handle his authenticity. It is a testimony to his faith.

Authenticity can breed change. Can we be a safe place for one another? Am I a safe place for friends to confide their feelings, fears, and doubts to? Pooh Bear, one of my favorite childhood characters, says, "A friend is someone who helps you up when you are down, and if they can't, they lay down beside you and listen." Authenticity is the spark needed for the fire of change to ignite. Change that we often need. And change is hard, but good change is worth learning the hard way, if that's what it takes.

I was down. I would be down a lot during the next several years, but God, our ultimate friend, was big enough to handle that. With him I never felt misunderstood. He is a safe place. He came for the discouraged, the lowly and for sinners. Mark 2:13-17 says,

> "He (Jesus) went out again beside the sea, and all the crowd was coming to him, and he was teaching them. And as he passed by he saw Levi the son of Alphaeus sitting at the tax booth, and he said to him, 'Follow me.' And he rose and followed him. And as he reclined at the table in his house, many tax collectors and sinners were reclining with Jesus and his disciples, for there were many who followed him. And the scribes of the Pharisees, when they saw that he was eating sinners and tax collectors said to his disciples, 'Why does he eat with tax collectors and sinners?' And when Jesus heard it, he said to them, 'Those who are well have no need of a physician, but those who are sick. I came not to call the righteous, but sinners.'"

Jesus knows how needy we are. Why was I trying to hide from him? I have spent a lot of intense days rolling around in the mud with the Lord. But as much as I want to shake my fist in the sky (and sometimes do), his gentle kindness reminds me that he was not (and is not) up in the fluffy, cotton-ball clouds looking down waiting to see if we will pass his tests. He doesn't do a condescending "head shake" when we don't wake up in the morning singing hymns and end the day with coffee and a women's bible study group. He is not like that. No, when I was sitting on my bed crying, feeling like the un-sexiest bald woman in the world, and I felt tired of feeling tired, he was sitting on the bed crying with me. Two years after learning I was cancer free, when I wept on the bathroom floor after starting my monthly cycle yet again, and when I hurled my phone at the sofa as hard as I could because I felt like I couldn't handle one more baby announcement on social media, and when I looked longingly at adoptive mothers in the church sanctuary and couldn't pay any attention to the sermon because of my aching heart, he had his arm tightly wrapped around my lonely shoulder. And he was crying too. *He was crying right beside me. He was crying with me.* My pain hurt his heart. It hurt his heart enough to make him cry too. God didn't abandon me in the dark . . . no, he was in it with me . . . full of compassion and tender love. Ready to sit there with me, arms locked with mine, for as long as it would take. And he is ready to do the same *for you*, dear one. I promise.

CHAPTER 12

A Sovereign Conversation

"But somewhere after the first five years of life in my wheelchair, I noticed
a change in my attitude toward hardships. I was beginning to see how my
quadriplegia was working for my good and God's glory-simply put, it meant
becoming more like Christ."

—JONI ERICSON TADA[1]

It was a late summer day. A dear friend had connected me to one of
the most motherly, infertile, God loving 50-year-old(ish) women she knew.
I had never met Macon before, but when I arrived at her house, she em-
braced me like we had known each other for years. She immediately made
me feel at ease with her warmth and genuine smile. She met me in her
driveway as I pulled up in my car. It was a warm, spring day. The sun was
shining brightly. Her neighborhood was full of tall, aged, luscious, green
trees. There was a refreshing breeze in the air. The cheery, peaceful setting
was a foreshadowing of the conversation in store. She had asked me in an
email if I would like to go for a walk with her around her neighborhood
and "talk."

I was a little nervous on my drive over. I was about to meet with a
woman that I didn't know to discuss a raw and pain filled topic. One that
was going to force me to be vulnerable to a stranger. But I trusted the friend

---

1. Tada. *God's Hand*. 1.

who introduced us. She encouraged me to connect with Macon, and here I was pulling into her driveway waving back at her warm welcome through my windshield. I was excited, too. To talk to a woman who had walked this path and was on the other side of its intense heat, strong and kind. A woman who has adopted several children and felt as passionate about adoption as I did. We not only had infertility in common, but we had a thirst to see lonely children put into families as well. I opened my car door with a nervous, excited anticipation. She hugged me tightly, as if we had known each other for years. She leashed her playful golden retriever, and we headed out the garage door for a walk that had meaty conversation in store. A depth of conversation that I wasn't quite expecting. A steak and potatoes type conversation. One that I would chew on for weeks and months to come. One that the Lord would use to change me forever.

God indeed used Macon that day to change my sorrow into dancing. As in, he spoke directly to me through her, and his words comforted my longing soul. And I knew that was what was happening, even in those moments. Our conversation felt "different." It felt divinely appointed. In some ways, it even felt epic, at least for me. As we strolled down the sidewalks of her lavish neighborhood, with the sun piercing through the giant, overgrown, green, full, tree branches I felt a sense of the Lord's brightness, love and peace shining through into my withered heart. A beauty knocking at the door, trying to enter in the dark spaces of my heart. Peace in the midst of heartache. I felt understood, unjudged, and hopeful. I soaked up conversations with other infertile women like a sponge. Especially women who had survived the heat of its grief, and were now thriving. Using their experiences with it as a ministry to other infertile women . . . just like Macon was doing to me. I felt hope peeking at me.

Our shared passion for the orphan also spurred passionate conversation that inspired me. In the middle of our conversation I was already dreading it coming to an end . . . wishing it could continue forever. Do you ever do that? Get tempted to miss the fullness of a moment because you are anticipating its end? I could have easily walked and talked with this woman for another three hours. She was a nurturer. Macon told me her story while on our walk. She started off with her story in an effort, I know, to make me feel comfortable. I could tell she was good at putting other people at ease. A talent she uses strategically to bless those around her. She is very much the mothering type. She told me her heart, and I was a stranger to her. "Ohhhhhh Catherineeeeeeee" she would always begin with after I would share something, in her very southern and "I understand," motherly way. "I didn't understand what was happening to me either, at the time," she shared, "but, now, now I can see." "I have four children who are my joy. The Lord had plans for me that I didn't have for myself. He has a plan for you, Catherine. I know you can't see it right now, but trust him, please, he is doing something here." She was vulnerable and open and honest and real and hopeful. She told me about her four children, each adopted and divinely appointed to be her beloved. She told me about the adoption agency that she and her husband had started in our city, using her lawyer experience as a springboard for its creation. She told me about her pain and her joys in motherhood. She told me about her faith in the goodness of God, even in the midst of heartache. I remember the word, *faith*, being used a lot. It was easy for me to receive that from her. She had walked this path. She knew, really knew from experience, what it felt like. Faith. "Hmm," I said, "I don't have much of that right now I feel like." Macon "Ohhhhh Catherineeeeee, it's okay, I do. I see God doing something."

One thing she shared resonated with me so strongly that I could not get it out of my head. Little did I know in that moment but it would become an anthem in my heart and on my lips for weeks, months, and years to come. She told me, "The plans of the Lord cannot be thwarted." And she said it with conviction . . . and she said it to me. And I heard her. I heard God telling me that through her. Proverbs 16:9 says "The heart of man plans his way, but the Lord establishes his steps." The plans of the Lord cannot be thwarted. I parked my heart in that spot for hours, days, and weeks to come. If the plans of the Lord really cannot be thwarted, then my husband's hesitancy towards adoption will not stop us, if it's the Lords will, I thought to myself. If the plans of the Lord really cannot be thwarted than William and I will conceive a child though the doctor's say it's impossible. If the plans of the Lord really cannot be thwarted than one hamburger or one milkshake or one thing off of my meal plan is not going to doom me to have a cancer relapse. If the plans of the Lord really can't be thwarted than maybe I should take a deep breath and relax into the arms of my Savior who is conducting this whole thing.

Driving away from her house that day, thinking on what she said about the plans of the Lord not being thwarted, I believed it. It was like, unbeknownst to me, the Holy Spirit had prepared my heart to hear that comforting news. The implications of the Lord's plans being unable to be thwarted bring an overflowing peace and encouragement that are real.

Whatever those plans mean for me. The fact that God has plans for me and I can trust him with them, causes me to not only rest, but rejoice. Cancer was hard, but it couldn't hold a candle to the pain of infertility. This pain is forever. Chemo had an end date. There was no end in sight to this situation. But God wasn't surprised. His plans cannot be thwarted. He knew all this was going to happen. God is never blindsided. What a comfort.

I have come to realize that there are so many things we learn through pain that we could not learn otherwise. God has taught me so much through it. Mostly, *my neediness creates relationship and a taste of his goodness that I could not know outside of the pain.* The pain drives me to his feet. Instead of feeling heartbroken and angry that day, I felt peace and comfort in the midst of the other emotions. My circumstances had not changed. I was childless. I could not conceive and my husband was not sure adoption was a path he wanted to pursue. Perhaps, the latter being even more painful than the inability to conceive. Two of my biggest dreams were still unfulfilled. And at that time, I didn't know what the future held. But God told me through Macon to *trust him.* His plans cannot be thwarted. And I knew it was real. And peace sprouted in my heart. A new thing was happening inside of me.

I have come to believe the Lord is sovereign. I think this is why I felt so angry at him for not doing what my heart longed for him to do in my womb. My anger only doubled when I could not understand why he didn't seem to be moving in the heart of my husband as I begged the Lord in private prayer to lead our family to adoption. My prayers seemed to be in vain. I spent many days beating my fist into the floor as I cried and begged God to do for us what he seemed to be doing for everyone else. I yelled at him through sobs as I drove alone in my car. I cried more tears than I knew my body could form. And he was catching each one, numbering them. Heartache was my closest friend. I couldn't understand his reasoning. As Hannah did in first Samuel, I wept bitterly. I questioned his goodness. Is he really good? Is he good to me?

Over time, I came to believe that he is good. Through tears shed at his feet behind closed doors, through prayers cried out to him as I lay on the bathroom floor in a snotty nose mess, through quietly reading his Word through eyes that were swollen and red, through being honest with the Lord as I grieved, and mainly through *realizing that the Lord neither enjoys nor wastes the suffering he calls us to.* His sovereignty and goodness go hand in hand. This then is what allows me to trust him. Nahum 1:7 says "The Lord is good, a stronghold in the day of trouble." Without him being good, he would be scary. I questioned if I really believed in his sovereignty and goodness when all I seemed to be getting was silence on the good things I was asking him to do.

He cares. He sees me. He knows that my heart aches to carry a child in my womb. He knows that I long to experience childbirth. He knows that I have always dreamed of being an adoptive mother. He knows my deep affection for Africa. He knows that I want to breastfeed. He knows that my heart wants to see William and myself in a child's eyes or hair or personality. He knows that I have dreamed of raising my children to be kind-hearted leaders who fight for justice and the outcast. He knows the desire I have had to take a child from an orphanage and bring him or her into my home as my own. He knows the way I long to watch my newborn's tiny fingers wrap around my own. He knows the kisses I have stored and dreamed of planting all over my adopted child's face. He knows all of these things. And yet, the plans of the Lord cannot be thwarted. And somehow, for me, him knowing these things, is enough. He hasn't abandoned me. This isn't all just some cold-hearted test. He is Emmanuel, God with us. And he is with us when we hurt. He is with you when you hurt. What are you hurting over, right now? Emmanuel, he is the one with you.

If God wills for us to have a biological child, we will. And if the Lord wills for us not to have a biological child, we won't. No matter what the doctor said. If God can impregnate a virgin, he can cause an infertile couple to conceive. If he wills for us to adopt then we will. If we wills for us not to, then we won't. If he can change the heart of Paul, he can change the heart of my hesitant husband, according to *his* will. "With man it is impossible, but not with God. For all things are possible with God" Mark 10:27. His plans will prevail despite what our limitations (or capabilities) are. We cannot create life and we cannot change hearts. This is the work of God alone. He is the giver, taker and sustainer of all life. The Great I Am. No matter the case, my heart will still sing of his sovereignty and goodness because I know he has plans that cannot be thwarted for my life. And he has plans that cannot be thwarted for *your life* too.

A hero of mine is Joni Ericson Tada. A Jesus loving woman bound to her wheelchair. Her quote below, I believe, sums up well, how suffering is not a waste but an avenue to the open, waiting arms of Jesus . . .

> ". . . I always say that in a way, I hope I can take my wheelchair to heaven with me—I know that's not biblically correct, but if I were able, I would have my wheelchair up in heaven right next to me

when God gives me my brand new, glorified body. And I will then turn to Jesus and say, 'Lord, do you see that wheelchair right there? Well, you were right when you said that in this world we would have trouble, because that wheelchair was a lot of trouble! But Jesus the weaker I was in that thing, the harder I leaned on you. And the harder I leaned on you, the stronger I discovered you to be. So thank you for what you did in my life through that wheelchair. And now,' I always say jokingly, 'you can send that wheelchair to hell, if you want.'

"That thought tickles me, but not long ago when someone heard me say that, they replied, 'Oh Joni. You can't mean that. Look at how God has changed you through your wheelchair. Look how close you've drawn to Jesus because of it. And look at the ministry that came through it and all the people reached. Please, don't say you want God to kick it out of heaven,' my friend said 'Why, the Lord just may transform it into something golden and glorious studded with beautiful jewels for every person you've reached for Christ through that wheelchair of yours.'

"And you know what? She had me. She stumped me. After all, the Bible does say that it has been given to us to suffer for his sake. My wheelchair is a gift from God—a gift! I never would've chosen this gift, but since God chose it for me, I'll take it as a gift, hard as though it may be at times. So there may be such a thing in heaven as holy wheelchairs . . . if God's throne has wheels, and the book of Daniel makes it crystal clear it does . . . then who am I to say that there won't be other chairs in heaven with wheels on them, too? Not to sit in, thank the Lord, but wheelchairs as symbols of the bruisings of a blessing that God has given people like me when he had blessed us with the gift of suffering.

"So, friend listening, if you are in a wheelchair, or using a walker, or a cane or crutch . . . try imagining it gilded and golden and encrusted in jewels. Oh, it's a strange and humorous picture, but remember, it is the gift that causes you to be weak—and the weaker you are, the stronger you will discover your Lord and Savior to be. More than 40 years in my wheelchair has taught me that—and in heaven, whether or not my old wheelchair is parked up there by the gates of pearl, feel free to join me in dropping on brand-new, grateful glorified knees before our Savior for all that he has done through our sufferings, yours and mine."[2]

So, I imagine my empty, unexpanded womb, in the words of Joni, "golden and encrusted in jewels." A gift.

2. https://www.epm.org/blog/2016/Nov/7/joni-suffering-sorrow-wheelchairs.

CHAPTER 13

Names and Faces

"Religion that is pure and undefiled before God the Father is this: to visit orphans and widows in their affliction, and to keep oneself unstained from the world."

—JAMES 1:27

I was nineteen years old and I had just completed my freshman year of college at UNC Chapel Hill. I was not, emphasis on the word *not*, interested in spending my first college summer participating in the North Carolina debutante debut and ball that I had been invited to. This was especially the case when I had been extended an invitation to go to Kenya, Africa to spend a month in an orphanage there. Adoption wasn't just a plan-B response to infertility for me, it was something I had been planning for since childhood. The decision between being a North Carolina debutante and going to Kenya for the summer was a no brainer for me. I was ready to be on the next plane out of the Raleigh-Durham International airport, Africa bound in heart and spirit. Sure, I could get my bags ready in time! Heck, do I even need a bag? Africa was a place my heart had been longing to visit since as long as I could remember. A place I would later learn was the dirt on which my children would be born. A place I could not wait to experience and see for myself. A place I had heard was unlike any other. A place that I knew then, and can testify to now, thirteen years later, always has and always will have a big piece of my heart. A place that, as I will explain later, would go from being one of my husband and I's biggest dividers, to one of our greatest unifiers.

Her name was Jane. And oh, how I remember her precious face. You would remember it too if you had seen it. Those soft, full cheeks, her puppy dog, brown eyes and her long, dark, cutely-styled braids. That sweet, little face that didn't smile one time during my month-long stay in the orphanage. A face that caused me to do a double take my first day walking inside of the, bow-and-arrow guarded, orphanage gates. Her eyes revealed a sadness in them that showed her life experiences greatly exceeded the three or four years of life that she had lived. And I knew, in my first moments having stepped foot inside the orphanage compound, red African clay on the soles of my sneakers, that I would learn more in my thirty days here than I had learned in the last nine months of my multi-thousand-dollar American, university experience. And the children, Alice included, would be my professors. She had been robbed. Robbed of something irreplaceable. Robbed of her early childhood. Her eyes were heavy, like they were carrying a load that was far too much for such a small frame.

There were so many kids. Each one with his or her own story. Each one there because of something traumatic that now separated them from their families. How and why they ended up at the Rafiki orphanage was different for each one. Some had similar stories, but each one stemmed from a unique and pain-filled brokenness. Being in this well-run, Bible-loving Rafiki orphanage meant hope and provision for each soul under its care. Rafiki means "friend" in Swahili. This place was a friend, not only to these orphaned and vulnerable children, but to all of its staff, missionaries, and the entire community.

Each of my new friends at the orphanage had his or her own talents, own preferences and own personalities. Each one with his or her own favorite color, favorite game, favorite subject in school. Each one had the capacity to give and receive love, some knew how to do that without guidance, others were too confused and burned by life to be able to do it freely . . . yet. I was experiencing the humanity of these orphans in a life altering type of way. I had the chance to experience, firsthand, that these orphans are people, little people. They are little people that desperately need love. Little people that need someone to lock arms with them and hope in them. Someone to share their dreams with and have someone to believe that they can accomplish those dreams. Someone to direct and guide them through life. Someone to tell them about the love, acceptance, healing and hope found in Jesus. Someone to share life with on a deep, rich and personal level. Someone to ask their questions to, the hard questions and the silly, innocent, child wonder type questions. They are little people that didn't choose this fate for themselves. They are little people who have endured so much loss in their few years. Much more than many of us will know in a lifetime. They are little people who are alone in this world. They are little people that will one day have to leave the orphanage gates. They are little people that grow into adults. And, without intervention, the majority of these hurting adults will (statistically) become criminals, prostitutes, or commit suicide. These children need the hope and healing of Jesus. They also need forever families.

Each child hopes for family, love, nurture, and acceptance, even if that can't be verbalized. And each child *deserves* it too. Each one. *Each and every one.* This trip made it abundantly clear to me that I was supposed to be that "someone" to one (maybe lots) of these little ones.

The children at the Rafiki Village in Kenya were well cared for by the leaders in the orphanage and the orphanage mothers, all of whom were widows. Heartbreak caring for heartbreak. I was so humbled to spend time with these warrior women and children. They are so brave, so strong, so faith-filled. The children were well fed, clothed, they attended school, medically cared for, and they were faithfully taught the Word of God. I remember Elijah, a precious deaf eight year old boy. He was given one-on-one daily care with a speech pathologist with many sessions ending in screaming fits of rage because of the overwhelming stimulation of first-time hearing aids and the daunting task of using his tongue to try and form coherent words. For years no one realized he was deaf; they thought he was quiet. These were the types of battles the children were facing. The list was long. And *God sees each one* and his or her needs . . . and desperately cares.

The children were taught Scripture and they put me to shame with the long passages of the Old Testament that they had memorized. The Bible was dear to this community. They challenged me to know it better. They challenged me to pray with faith the way that they prayed with faith. They deeply depended on God for their needs. I will never forget the cottage mothers' fervent prayers in a morning, adult-only devotional time. They asked God to send rain to their gardens so that they would have enough food. When is the last time we have had to pray to God to have enough food? I was frozen in that moment, stunned (and dare I say) jealous even at their dependence on the Lord. A moment I believe the Lord ordained to brand on my heart to serve me as I walked through the trials that lay ahead for me in years to come. A moment that indeed was branded on my heart, and I was reminded of many times when I struggled trusting God. The children knew every verse to hymns such as "Great is Thy Faithfulness" and "It is Well with My Soul." These songs were sung with passion. I wanted more of what they had. They had dependence. They had spiritual wealth. It was, no doubt, manifested through the trials they had both endured and survived. The prosperity Gospel wasn't on their radar. God was their source of wealth and strength and provision and hope. It was beautiful. Absolutely beautiful. I was convicted. *I wanted more of what their spirits had.*

The children were such kids. They played hard. Rolling tires, playing soccer, being pushed on the swings, braiding each other's hair and playing tag were just a few of the ways they spent their free time and burned off energy stores that never seemed to deplete. This was the first time I spent an extended time around so many children. I loved every minute of it. This was a safe place. A new environment for many of the kids. They did not need to worry about where the next meal was coming from. The adults would take care of that. They were given permission to be kids, wild and free, for some, for the first time ever. It would take time for some of them to learn that, but this place offered them that security. They did not need to worry. Kids could be kids here; adults would take care of their needs. This was a luxury many had never known. A luxury I had grown up expecting. I was so moved by their stories. Their grit. Their faith.

I never did see little Jane smile or speak. She was quiet, obedient, and easy to be around. She was a very sweet-natured little girl. Clearly though, she was hurting. I don't know how Jane got there. I don't know if she ever knew her birth parents, if she watched them pass away, if they were killed, if she was abandoned and spent time on the ruthless streets, if they were alive and wanted to provide for her but couldn't . . . I don't know any of that. But I do know this one thing—she is *special*. She is a gift to the world. Jane pierced my heart. Even now as I sit here typing this, I can see the softness of her full, brown cheeks. Her oversized clothes, and her long, beautiful, heavy braids. Her hands, face, toes, and eyes were molded by the very hands of God. She is his beautiful masterpiece. As a potter shapes his art on a wheel, so God crafted Jane. He chose to color her eyes that shade of brown and her lips a soft pink. Food and shelter and education were a blessing. Those things meant survival. The education may have even meant future prosperity. But Jane needed more than that. Jane needed a family.

This summer trip to this orphanage after my first year of college, changed me forever. I had dreamed of adopting since I was a little girl, but it wasn't until I stayed in that orphanage and got to know the children individually, that I began to put names and faces with the term "orphan." Each child comes from a different situation. *Relationships change the way you view things.* Suddenly, those "orphans" had names and faces and likes and dislikes and personalities and talents and struggles. Each one so unique and special. Each one with his or her own story. Each one deserving of love.

David Platt says, "We learned that orphans are easier to ignore before you know their names. They are easier to ignore before you see their faces. It is easier to pretend they're not real before you hold them in your arms. But once you do, everything changes."[1]

This trip ignited something inside of me for pleading the case of the underprivileged. God calls his followers to do this. Sometimes it is hard to know how to do it most effectively. I have also come to realize that it can be easy to overthink it. Do you ever find yourself in that place? It's easy to make things overly complicated, become overwhelmed and walk away doing, risking, and trying nothing. My dear, Jesus-adoring friend and (she doesn't know it) mentor, Cindy, says, "Just because you can't do everything, doesn't mean you can't do nothing." Overanalyzing can be dangerous because it causes us to never move into action. *Faith has to act.* I have learned that prayer is key. God will show us what he wants us to do to be involved in caring for these vulnerable children. Then we can jump in, no dive in, head first. I was waiting on my green light from the Lord. It was clear I didn't have it yet. But I was ready to leap and dive when he was ready to give it. If he would only?

1. Platt. *Radical.* 139.

CHAPTER 14

Wait on Me

"Answer me quickly, O Lord! My spirit fails! Hide not your face from me, lest
I be like those who go down to the pit. Let me hear in the morning of your
steadfast love, for in you I trust. Make me know the way I should go, for to you
I lift up my soul."

—PSALM 143:7-8

Adoption was not something that William, my best friend/make
out partner, always wanted to do. I mentioned this briefly in earlier chap-
ters. Actually, truth be known, it was something we did not see eye-to-eye
on for a long time. It wasn't that he didn't believe in adoption or think that
it was a good thing. He did. But he personally didn't feel a strong desire to
do it. He was actually quite opposed to the idea of us pursuing adoption.
With his permission, this is his story, unfiltered and raw. I share it with
the intention of displaying the power of God to transform hearts and to
encourage other men feeling the same hesitancies. Which I have learned
through many open and honest conversations with other couples is common. Transparency breeds change.

    Earlier in our relationship my desire to adopt would irritate William.
In fact, during our college dating years we nearly broke up over it. I was
adamant. He was "open" but not sure, and certainly not passionate about it
like I was. He was not willing to commit to pursuing it, all the while I was
begging for him to sign on the dotted line. . . . ahem . . . in blood, please.

We talked it through and decided to stay together, despite our differing thoughts on the topic. We were believing that God would put us on the same page about his will for our lives, including adoption. We believed that we were supposed to be together. William couldn't understand why I was so passionate about *us* adopting. I couldn't understand why he wasn't. It was one of the few areas we weren't aligned. Our passions and hobbies tended to align, this was a big area that we didn't. I hated that.

William assumed I wanted to adopt because it was a popular "Christian trend." If it is a fad, he wants no part of it. He is a genuine human being. He loves Jesus. He is honest (sometimes a little bit too honest). It is something that I have grown to appreciate about him. Regardless, I would often feel hurt after our discussions about adoption. I would feel hurt that my motives were being questioned, and I would feel a sense of panic that this adoption longing might go unfulfilled. A longing that I wholeheartedly believed had been placed in my heart by God. A longing I was trying to convince my husband was God's will for us. A longing I was trying to make sure came to fruition. A longing I was too scared to loosen my grip on and lay before the Lord because relinquishing control like that freaked me out . . . then it *really* might not happen!

We had our fair share of heated conversations around the subject. These discussions only intensified after learning that we would not be able to have biological children. William had always told me that he would like for us to have biological children first, then we would consider adoption one day "down the road." When I learned that we wouldn't be able to have biological children, my passion for adoption only seemed to grow bigger. I actually told the Lord one day in a grieving prayer that I really wanted both biological and adopted children, but if I could only have one, I choose to be an adoptive mother. The longing for that was honestly stronger. The threat of not having this dream fulfilled made my fear shoot off like a rocket. Too high to be measured, too scared to spend much time considering it not happening.

I spent days, months and years begging God to put William and I on the same page about this passion. But even after learning that we would not have biological children, William's feelings remained the same towards adoption. He wasn't sure this was something that he wanted to do. *I was panicking on the inside.* I thought, "God, don't do this to me. Don't let this longing go unfulfilled too." This longing that may rock me even more than the loss of my forever empty womb if left unfulfilled. One day, by God's clear leading in a time of quiet one-on-one time with the Lord, I decided not to bring up the adoption topic again despite the fact that my heart was absolutely *aching* for it. Like, he told me to *never* ever bring it up again. I freaked out, and committed that I would *not* bring it up. I absolutely knew this is what God was telling me to do. I was *very afraid* to do this. I felt afraid that God was going to withhold another dream from me. Dare I say, an even bigger dream, and thus, a potentially even bigger loss. For a former control addict like myself, this was a major test in surrender. Is surrender something that you fear? It is so scary, right? God was telling me to have faith in him, in his goodness, and in *his will* for my life. But what if his will is not my will? Have you been there? It's an honest question. It's a scary place. He told me to stop trying to make things go my way using my "power." He told me to stop trying to manipulate and guilt trip my husband to get what I wanted. To get what I believed was the Lord's will for our family. He was telling me to let him be God to my husband. He was telling me to stop playing the Holy Spirit. I was adamant that I did not want to be a nagging wife who convinced her husband to do things that he really didn't want to do, especially something as life altering as adoption. I was on the brink (that may be a gracious personal assessment, ah-hem) of becoming a nagging wife that I genuinely did not want to be. I didn't know how to stop though. I wanted to adopt! What if I don't bring it up anymore and this dream floats unfulfilled into the heavens like a balloon into the deep, blue sky, only before popping and being gone forever? What if my dream goes unfulfilled forever? What if I lose this too? I'll die, I thought. "No you won't," the Lord reassured me. *"You have me."*

Have *FAITH*, God told me. My trusted friend , Abigail . . . again . . . Ha! I see a pattern with the truth she speaks into my life . . . wisely suggested that God would lead me through leading my husband. This is the same wise friend that suggested that maybe God ordained my cancer rather than just allowing it to happen. I am so thankful for this mentor. She is as bold as she is wise.

It was time, past time actually, for me to demonstrate that I really believed what I said I believed . . . that if God wanted us to adopt, he would put William and I on the same page about it.

That if God wanted us to adopt there would be unity between us about it. Did I really believe this? Or did I actually believe it was up to me to convince William of what God was telling us to do? Can you relate, at all? This unknown is a scary place to be when you are talking about something so close to your heart. To go without this would be to lead a life I never envisioned for myself. I knew adoption was a part of my DNA. Ironic, eh? The plans of the Lord cannot be thwarted.

Though I did not bring it up to my husband any more after making my decision that day, I did bring it up to God. I brought it up to God a lot. A whole lot. I prayed about it harder than I have ever prayed about anything else. I prayed about it . . . on the ground . . . on my face . . . daily . . . sometimes hourly. These moments transpired behind a closed door, often through sobs. I felt like I was grieving the loss of biological children and grieving the potential loss of the dream of adoption back to back. And I was doing it in the secret, with the Lord. *I really did believe that God had put this desire in my heart.* I can honestly say that I wanted it more than I have ever wanting anything in my entire life. I prayed that God would take the desire to adopt away if it wasn't his will for our family. I knew that there were other ways to care for orphans, but the desire *did not* go away. It didn't go away at all. In fact, *it grew bigger* inside of me. "Great," I thought. I was seriously frustrated. This would be so much easier, if the desire would just dissipate, I thought to myself. I felt frustrated at the Lord. Ok God, I thought, William is your son and you are his God. If you want this for us, then show him. Not me. *You.* You show him. I'm not getting in the middle of this anymore.

So, I continued to pray. In relinquishing (faux) control, I found real dependence. A dependence I had only scratched the surface of with the cancer. A dependence I had delved deeper into as I grieved my empty womb. I was needy during this season. I was a needy mess. I was like a tiny child looking to mommy to help me sit up, and dress me, and feed me, and wipe me, and do it all. And I was doing it in secret, away from my husband, my dearest friend. *In this neediness I strangely found freedom.* The burden to adopt became weightier on my heart, but the fear of it not happening melted as I began to melt into the safe, big, strong arms of Jesus. Peace began to creep in. His arms were muscular enough to carry this burden for me. And so I began to let him. Cancer and infertility had been my training ground in surrender. I wasn't angry or hurt. I wasn't bitter at William. I surprisingly felt very close to him. I didn't have to manipulate my husband to get what I thought God wanted for us. If God wanted this for our family wouldn't he show him? Isn't he God? Isn't he capable of that? The pressure was off me. God had confirmed to me this was his will. I was certain, because he told me, so in time he would tell my husband the same thing. I had to pray and trust God to be God to me, and to be God to my husband.

During this season of intense prayer and dependency I learned that I needed to be changed. I, for maybe the first time, held the adoption desire open handed before the Lord. I examined my heart before the Lord. I examined God's heart for orphans. I looked at God's command to care for the weak, the defenseless, the vulnerable. *I realized I had been loving the idea of adoption more than I had been loving the God who had adopted me.* I had been taking a good thing, a thing close to his heart, and valuing it more than I treasured him. God really used that season for me to examine my own heart. I was convicted. I started to try to know more of him for him. Not him for what he could give me. Nor him for the good things I knew he loved. And I was convicted to wait on this all-powerful God to lead and grow our family as he saw fit. I didn't have to panic and feel out of control for the thing my heart was idolizing. I could lay it at Jesus' feet, seek to know God for himself, and trust him to lead my husband.

As I mentioned, God was unmistakably clear to me, "the desire to adopt is there for a reason. I put it there. Wait on me." So I did. I did, however, ask the Lord for an answer by a specific date, July 31st, 2016, William's 29th birthday. A spiritually sound thing to do, I don't know. Right or wrong to do, I don't know. But I did it. I did it with faith. So I prayed and I waited and confessed my sin. Every day. The patience (not a natural gift of mine) and dependence (again, I'm not a natural at this . . . more of a go-get-'em, take the bull by the horns type) that I learned during this three month season changed my heart forever. I was so convicted of how judgmental I had been. I was convicted of how I try to control other people, not just William, to get my way. I was convicted about my pushiness. I had been too busy judging than to have faith in God and his unstoppable plans for our lives. I had been too busy idolizing my desire to adopt rather than loving the God who has adopted me. The God who changes hearts, something no man can do. The God who was changing my heart. And the God, who, unbeknownst to me, was changing my husband's heart as well.

CHAPTER 15

A Heart That Was Changed

"We instinctively know that love leads to commitment, so we look away when we see a beggar. We might have to pay if we look too closely and care too deeply. Loving means losing control of our schedule, our money, and our time. When we love we cease to be the master and become a servant."

—PAUL MILLER[1]

It was a regular day . . . or so I thought. It's interesting to look back on our lives and dog-ear the pages that we expected to be regular yet were firework shows instead. Those are the days my friend, Brenda, currently battling a rare form of sinus cancer, calls "Ebenezer days." These are the days that we mark in our hearts and minds with our highlight pen of life. Days of remembrance that build our faith in monumental ways. Days we are not to forget. Days we can look back as wells to draw strength from on the days our faith feels flimsy.

    William and I had both been to work, and now I was at home preparing dinner. Cooking continues to be one of my favorite ways to decompress from a long day. There is something about the way the steam warms my face and the way mindlessly chopping veggies calms my mind. I usually play soft, classical music in the background as the sautéing veggies and boiling water sing to the same beat as the music in my dimly, often, candle

1. Miller. *Love Walked.* 32.

lit kitchen. William came home and, after eating, we needed to ride out to Home Depot (likely for another gardening tool for-what felt like to us-our mini farm at that time). But honestly, I cannot remember what it was specifically that we were going for. When you live in the middle of nowhere, a ride out to Home Depot can feel like a real night out on the town! I looked forward to our rides into town to stock on needed supplies. Anyway, we rode out in William's beloved 2007 Toyota Tacoma, a truck so cherished by its owner that I tease him about where I fall in the lineup for his affection. A joke he shakes his head at with his usual "oh hush" side smile while reaching for my hand.

We had parked outside of Home Depot and before opening the car doors to go inside William said to me out of nowhere, "Do you think that God is telling us to adopt?"

Taken back by the randomness and magnitude of the question (considering my secret time with the Lord over the past three months), I paused, felt my heart-rate go up and said, "Yes, I do."

William: "I think that we are supposed to adopt too."

Heart-rate now soaring to dangerous levels, wide eyed, I respond, "Really?"

William: "Yes." He went on to explain to me, in great detail, how he felt like God had totally changed his heart on the matter, and he didn't know why exactly. Like totally changed his heart! He spoke open hearted and tenderly towards the subject. Something that he had never done before. He talked about it with a longing in his voice that I was blown away by. He said that God has adopted us into his family, why wouldn't we do this as a response to him. Plus, these children who have been orphaned needed homes and we could provide that. He said these children didn't choose this life for themselves. He asked how selfish would we have to be to not take care of them? How could he say no to God, who was unmistakably telling him to do this?

I was blown away. Mouth ajar, eyebrows raised, tears welling up in my eyes, I sat, stunned at the things he was saying. Wow, Lord, was all I could think. I could have probably sat in the truck a few hours and cried, but William reminded me that we had come to Home Depot to get something, so we went inside. Man on a mission. I held his hand as we walked around the store, lost in the awe of God's power as I stared blankly at the incredibly vast number of light bulb choices. I was so moved by God's clear speaking to my husband. I had had no part in William reaching this decision. No coercive part I should say. Just prayer and faith in the God who can do whatever he wants in the heart of a person and a family. Later that evening, when we got home, I showed William my prayers I had written in my journal over the last three months. He read through my asking God for an answer to the nagging adoption question mark in my heart by July 31st. It was July 28th that day. William too was blown away, not knowing that these prayers were being prayed. Not realizing the agony of soul I had been having in the secret with the Lord. God used this to solidify to us that this was *indeed* his will for our family. We both felt so humbled, worship-filled, peaceful and excited about moving forward. We were both in awe of the Lord's power. We were now united in a way we had never been . . . and it was sweet.

A couple of months later, as we tried to figure out where God was calling us to adopt from, William came home with a serious look on his face. We knew that God was calling us to international adoption, but that doesn't quite narrow it down enough to move forward. Asia, Eastern Europe, Philippines, Africa, South America? Where, Lord? There are so many places where the need is great. All of these children need homes. William said that we needed to talk. This is unusual because he usually walks in the door and after a quick kiss on the cheek (if I'm lucky), it's a beeline for the pantry to eat around a thousand calorie snack before dinner is ready. (Side note: how can he do that and stay so thin? Dinner can literally be on the table and he will still go to the pantry to get a snack first. Really? I don't understand. He knows that it drives me crazy, but he does it anyway. Eye roll emoji here please).

We sat down together in the den for what I knew was a face-to-face conversation about something serious, which was different than our usual after work chit-chat. He told me that while he was working out in the gym that day, he believed God had told him that we were supposed to adopt a child from Africa, Ethiopia specifically. The conversation that then ensued between him and God while he was rolling on the elliptical, was apparently, according to William, a pretty intense one. He said that he had been praying, and the Holy Spirit impressed on him, in a heavy and unmistakable way, that Ethiopia was the country where our child was. Having traveled to Africa a couple of times (once with William) and having a love for Africa that I have never been able to explain, Ethiopia having been a place I had always dreamt of visiting (yet never told William this), my heart was again amazed at the Lord. This longing was placed in my heart by God, and now

God had placed it in my husband's heart too *and he was the one initiating it all!*

I was amazed at God's plans for our lives unfolding before me. These plans were not forced by my hand. I was on the side lines watching and marveling. These plans I had believed with all of my heart were his will for us, but felt so utterly confused and frustrated at him about previously. The way a flower woos a bee, so the Lord wooed us both into *his story for us.* And it felt right. *The plans of the Lord cannot be thwarted.* Amen. What is his story for you? He will reveal it, dear one. He will align the stars to make it happen . . . according to his will for you. Believe, pray, and cling to the promise that his plans for you are right and good and beyond your wildest imagination. God's plans *for you* cannot be thwarted! And you can dog-ear that day as an Ebenezer day, indeed.

William is a straight-forward man. Not a man of many words. Not a man of a lot of fluff. A kind-hearted man. I'd be lying if I said he doesn't have a little bit of an edge to him. He says what he means and he means what he says. He is direct with the ability to be oh so tender. He is full of so many opposites that he confuses a lot of people. He is both quiet and out-spoken. He is laid back and intense. He is kind and harsh. He is funny and serious. He is methodical and simple. He is humble and extremely confident. He doesn't change for other people. When he told me that he wasn't sure he wanted to adopt, he meant it. When he told me he wanted us to adopt, he meant it. When he told me that it was from Ethiopia, that was that. When he has a strong conviction about something, there is no changing his mind. Once he had a change of heart about adoption, he was all in. Stubborn as a dern' mule.

My husband has been more engaged and involved in our adoption journey than I have. He has researched, prayed, and been enraged by the injustice he has discovered about many children's stories. He now, as I am writing this, wants to adopt more children, and we have not yet brought our first daughter home (though we getting close!). We are on this adoption journey together, one hundred percent together. I am so grateful. I am amazed at the power of God to change hearts. *No man can change another man's heart. God can though, and only God, and he does. God does change hearts. And he is unstoppable.* His plans *for you,* are unstoppable. I will say it again, and again, the plans of the Lord cannot be thwarted!

CHAPTER 16

Walking into Darkness

"In him we have redemption through his blood, the forgiveness of our trespasses, according to the riches of his grace."

—EPHESIANS 1:7

As we embarked on the adoption journey, beginning mid-summer 2018, I quickly began to recognize the *many* layers of brokenness in this realm. They were discovered one layer at a time the further we delved into the lengthy, paperwork consuming process. I knew that adoption stems from trauma and pain, but I definitely did not realize the amount of child trafficking and abuse that is often times involved in international adoption. It is truly disturbing. As I learned more about the realities of the abuse, I became angry, confused and uncertain on how to be involved. To describe it briefly, in many third world countries adoption is a huge source of revenue for the country. Corrupt, evil people will go into cities and villages and kidnap children from their birth families that want them. They then will lie to orphanage staff and government officials by telling them made up stories of how they came to find the child. They will also make empty promises to poor, caring birth parents about how they will provide schooling, food, and clothing for the child in another city and then send the child home for visits. These are often lies, and the birth parents selflessly give their child over to a different life that will yield more opportunities never to see their beloved child again. It's heartbreaking. Needless to say, we were stunned when we learned this. We had just begun the adoption journey and we were scared and confused as to how to move forward. We sensed intense spiritual warfare. Should we be involved in something that we can't always have total certainty about things we are being told? We researched. We made phone calls to older, wiser friends who had walked the adoption path before us. We prayed. We kept praying. And then we prayed some more. We asked God to show us how to move forward. How to be sure that we weren't in any way contributing to child trafficking. We came across quite a few articles and blogs that had passionate opinions about how we should approach these issues as prospective adoptive parents, wanting to do the right thing. There are people with (strong) opinions on both ends of the spectrum. Some well-meaning people will say you should never adopt internationally because of all the ethical "what ifs" of adoption. On the other end of the spectrum you have well-meaning people say you need not pay any attention to the ethical "what ifs" because all children are better off in America. We agree with neither of these views.

We came to the conclusion that we should still be involved with international adoption, but we should not enter into any decision, even the small ones, in the process lightly. We resolved to research and question our adoption agency with shrewdness, to cover each step of the process in serious prayer. So, this is what we did. We prayed. We prayed a lot. We got access to a list of questions from our church's website on how to question your adoption agency regarding these issues. Our agency's answers to our extensive questioning gave us confidence that they are ethical in how they deal with government officials and orphans overseas. This was very helpful to us. No red flags. We felt peace and decided to move forward in faith.

Part of the reason we felt so stressed was because we owed our adoption agency four thousand dollars in a few short days in order to continue moving forward. I learned through this very stressful two week period leading up to that nonrefundable fee, at the end of the day, you have to do what God is laying on your heart. People will always have their opinions. People will often feel at liberty to share those opinions with you. However, *God will lead you if you ask him.* Prayer is everything. His peace is your clear answer on what to do. "You will seek me and find me when you seek me with all of your heart." Jeremiah 29:13

God deeply cares for these children who are living in orphanages, foster homes, refugee camps, on the streets and without families. He deeply cares for their past hurts their present hopes. These children, who need someone to fight on their behalf, to be their voice, to plead their case, are *deeply loved by our Father*. They are seen by our Father. They are not forgotten. And you know what? *You are too.* He deeply cares for you too. He sees your heart. Adoption is a beautiful showcase of how he chooses to weave stories together to create a really beautiful masterpiece.

I am not adopting because we can't have biological children. Many people do, and that is fine, even good. Yes, infertility did lead us to begin the adoption process sooner than expected, but it has always been a dream, a deep longing of mine. For as long as I can remember I have always had a deep longing for adopted children . . . shoes no biological child could never fill.

Adoption isn't about the parents. It is about God. God has a tender spot for the poor, the fatherless, the widow, and the souls that cannot defend themselves. Psalm 146:5-9 says "Blessed is he whose help is the God of Jacob, whose hope is in the Lord his God, who made heaven and earth, the sea, and all that is in them, who keeps faith forever; who executes justice for the oppressed, who gives food to the hungry. The Lord sets the prisoners free; the Lord opens the eyes of the blind. The Lord lifts up those who are bowed down; the Lord loves the righteous. The Lord watched over the sojourners; he upholds the widow and the fatherless, but the way of the wicked he brings to ruin." We see the Lord's heart for the fatherless and vulnerable all throughout his Word. Here are a few, of many, examples . . .

"For he will deliver the needy who cry out, the afflicted who have no one to help. He will take pity on the weak and the needy and save the needy from death. He will rescue them from oppression and violence, for precious is their blood in his sight." Psalm 72:12-14 (NIV)

"Learn to do good; seek justice, correct oppression; bring justice to the fatherless, plead the widow's cause." Isaiah 1:17

"If anyone has material possessions and sees a brother or sister in need but has no pity on them, how can the love of God be in that person? Dear children, let us not love with words or speech but with actions and in truth." 1 John 3:17 (NIV)

"Speak up for those who cannot speak for themselves, for the rights of all who are destitute. Speak up and judge fairly; defend the rights of the poor and needy." Proverbs 31:8-9 (NIV)

Adoption is about redemption. A child would always be best being in his or her birth parents' loving care. There are times when, for many different reasons, that isn't feasible. I have found that the tragedy and beauty woven into adoption is almost too much to take in. Adoption is a picture of taking a child that comes from a shattered situation and *providing forever family. Just as God has done for me. Just as God has done for you.* And how delighted he is to bring this beauty from ashes. How humbling it is to be a part of such sacred redemption.

CHAPTER 17

Baby Talk

"People who really want to make a difference in the world usually do it, in one way or another. And I've noticed something about people who make a difference in the world: They hold the unshakeable conviction that individuals are extremely important, that every life matters. They get excited over one smile. They are willing to feed one stomach, educate one mind, and treat one wound."

—BETH CLARK[1]

"Are you going to get a baby? I hope you get a new baby," I was told too many times to count. It was said from a place of love. People thinking about William and I and our comfort. Regardless, each time I heard it my heart would sink and I would feel a surge of disillusionment rise up inside of me. Right or wrong, I couldn't deny that it bothered me. I would fight to contain it and try not to make it obvious. I knew they were trying to love me, but the "are you going to get a baby?" questions can be so disheartening. I know it was people's way of wanting us to experience the early stages of our child's life. It was them wanting us to not have to "deal with" the extra baggage that comes from a life of early childhood trauma: homelessness, survival, starvation, war, abuse, and the list goes on. Regardless of their intentions, I always wanted to ask those people, "What if that were you?" (and sometimes did, hoping now it was done in a gentle way). What if that was me? Is

1. Clark. *Kisses from Katie.* X1

every life not valuable? Babies are cute, cuddly, and have less baggage than an older child, but does that mean we don't consider the older child? This is what would break my heart when I was petitioned with the baby question. What if I was left abandoned as a four year old and now lived in an orphanage? What if I had been the one living on the street trying to survive as a five year old? What if my parents had died of AIDS in my arms when I was ten? What if I had held my mother as an eight year old and watched her take her last breath, only to be left alone? What if I was a six year old acting as the primary caregiver of my two year old sister or brother, or both?

The younger the child, the less baggage adoptive parents have to deal with, so we are told. That may be true, but children also don't choose to be orphans, the babies nor the toddlers nor the school age nor the teenagers. *Every child matters. Every child matters to God, and therefore, every child should matter to us. Each one, in their very own stage, with their very own story, needs a home. Needs love. Needs the hope and healing of Jesus. Needs a family that will not give up on them. Needs parents to lock arms with them and be their cheerleader. Needs someone rooting for them saying you can do this. Needs parents that can walk with them through life's hard questions, point them to Jesus, and wait and watch him heal the very dark corners of their souls.*

I liked the idea of a younger child, especially since we had never been parents before, but William and I were also open to the idea of an older child. Or at least that is what we said. Our hearts *truly* opened to this after we were faced with a potential older child adoption opportunity. It drove us to prayer, the on our knees and faces type prayer. *Dependency.* I had said I was open to an older child. When I was actually met with the opportunity, I got scared. I felt like, I don't know how to be a mother to any child, much less a school age child who doesn't speak the same language I speak. She was almost eight years old. She was sick with HIV infection and needed medical attention. She had a soft smile and kind eyes. Her eighteen-year-old teenage sister was no longer able to take care of her now that their parents were both gone. I was only twenty-seven years old and I felt like a child, only a few short years away from puberty, was out of my league. The reality of potentially becoming a mother to a nearing middle schooler sunk in and drove me to my knees. I felt terrified. My heart needed searching. I lifted my trembling hands up to the Lord, after sitting on them first, too scared to lift them up in an act of true surrender. What my lips spoke of the Lord was being tested for its authenticity. Lip service about leaving your comfort zone and then *actually doing* something out of your comfort zone are two very different things. I bowed my head while he pried my fingers open before him. William and I both did. *I might say* that older children need a home, but was *I willing to do it?* Or was I just talk?

God really forced me to consider my true motives for adopting . . . to look into the secret corners of my self-adoring heart. Was I only willing to say yes to the Lord in the areas that made me excited, the areas that I felt comfortable? Can you be afraid and have his peace fill your heart at the same time? Yes, you totally can. Fleshly fear plus heavenly peace births courage. Was I willing to follow his call for us? William was. Was I only willing to give a partial yes to his call? *Is a partial yes really a no to the Lord?* I pondered these things in my heart. Was I only willing to give a yes based on my terms? What was he calling us to? My head was spinning with fear and confusion. "Is this our child, Lord?" I asked.

Becoming a parent to an adoptive child is weird in the sense that, in some capacity, you "pick out" your child. You, as the adoptive parent, have the right to "accept" or "reject" any referral. Biological parents don't do this. Choosing your children is not a natural thing to do. There is a strong temptation to believe that their fate rests on your decision. It can be a very heavy weight to carry. This way of thinking is wrong, but it's lure is there. It's easy to feel like if you don't accept this referral this child won't get a home, a family, a cheering squad, an inheritance and a love that will last forever. It brings you to the end of yourself and you have to trust that God is their provider, not you. This is what I was struggling with. Intense feelings of guilt mixed with a muddy-watered-heart mixed with confusion on how to move forward. He is the captain of their destiny, William reminded me. He cares for each one. His tender love abounds for these children. This is what God was showing me. God spoke to us as we sought him. "Draw near to God, and he will draw near to you." James 4:8. The Lord *told me that he didn't reject us because we were older, sick, traumatized, or broken.* Over the next several days my heart was truly changed. God met me in my neediness, fear and feelings of inadequacy. I can say with upmost sincerity that William and I both opened our hands before the Lord and said, with trembling and honest hearts, "Thy will be done."

After that experience, we decided that we were genuinely open to any child that he had for us. And we meant it. It wasn't just lip service anymore. We had been faced with an opportunity that didn't work out, but we had been willing. God was testing the purity of my heart in this process. He spoke to me in a tangible way during that three day stint (we had been given the weekend to consider the older child referral before we had to let the adoption agency know of our decision the following Monday). We honestly told God we would adopt an older child if that was what he wanted us to do. We also told him we would adopt a sick child if that was what he wanted us to do. I had told God that Down Syndrome was one thing I could not do. God told me to rethink that and consider why I was "unable" to do this for him.

When I considered it more, in prayer, I realized that my "no, not that" attitude was doubt in his provision for our family's future. Jesus not only didn't avoid the sick, he pursued them. Some medical needs, some ages, may be harder than others, *but God told me that hard is ok. He is the God who meets us in the hard. He is the God who can handle the hard.* The thought still scared me some (ok, a lot), but I meant it when I told God to grow our family according to *his* will. All I asked for was peace about it. Even if it looked overwhelming and out of my comfort zone, I just wanted peace from him as a way to know it was him building our family. And God used this time, this soul searching to teach me about his heart for *adopting me.* He has adopted me. I am his beloved daughter. In Christ, his identity is branded on me *forever.* I remind myself not to fall into the trap of thinking I am too broken for him. That I am too much work for him. That I am too messy for him. I'm not. And *you* aren't either! *We are exactly who he has chosen.*

Within twenty-four hours of the older child adoption not working out, we got another referral (pretty rare to get another referral so quickly I have come to learn). William and I both opened the file and immediately knew this was our daughter. We read her bio and looked at her picture and peace overflowed. *This child is our daughter.* We reached for each other's hands while our eyes remained glued to the screen, absolutely smitten by her. My head fell into William's shoulder, tears of joy rolled down our cheeks. That's our babe, we both said. We stared at the picture for hours, studying her every detail. It's as if the Lord blessed our honest seeking of his face. And there she was, our longed for, treasured, precious daughter. And we had peace. And this peace made us send an immediate reply to our agency-yes! This is our child. Our daughter. She is a Rackley.

As the adoption process kept moving in a forward direction, I continued to ask God to cause a child to form in my womb. I still do. I pray for this regularly. I must admit that I hope that it does not ever happen as we are in the middle of an adoption journey (I know there are more adoption journeys that lie ahead as William and I now hope *together* to adopt more children) as this would cause our adoption to be slowed down until the biological child was born, but I do pray regularly for a biological child to also be a part of our growing family.

Adoption will never replace the longing I have to carry a child in my womb. Having a child born from my womb will never replace my desire to adopt.

These two dreams are neither transferable nor interchangeable. They are not the same thing and they never will be. They are separate dreams. Two separate longings. Two separate callings. They both induce parenthood, but because you are infertile doesn't automatically mean you adopt, just as the ability to conceive children does not mean that you don't adopt.

For as long as I can remember I have always longed to both adopt and to carry a child in my womb. In fact, as I admitted earlier, the desire for an adopted child has always slightly trumped my desire for biological children . . . was this the Lord preparing me, even as a child? I never realized my innate hope to carry a child in my womb until that assumed privilege became a loss realized. I know God is still able to do this if he chooses. He is somehow able to take our ashes and turn them into something beautiful. He is unstoppable. This is the God who changes hearts. He is in the business of doing the impossible. *When the brokenness of life is real, God is able to bring beauty out of it.* He is able to do this for the teenage orphan and the infant orphan. He is able to do this for my aching womb. I believe this mystery is one of the things that makes him the most beautiful. Its kind, it's tender, *it's redemption.*

And we are all in need of it.

CHAPTER 18

Worth the Wait

"I am sure that God keeps no one waiting
unless he sees that it is good for him to wait."

—C.S. LEWIS[1]

Waiting is a hard thing to do. We all, at some point, have to wait. I don't even like typing that, or acknowledging how true it is. Waiting can be heart-wrenching. It demands patience. Trust. Hope. Faith. Things we don't feel capable of giving when our hearts are in a state of longing. So many different scenarios come to mind. The wife that waits for her husband to return home from deployment. The mother who waits for her addicted child to finally stop using after years of asking God for this. The infertile couple that waits for that second pink line to appear on their home pregnancy test month after month, year after year. The ill patient who waits to feel strong and full of life again. The orphan who waits to have a family to call his or her own. Why do we have to wait? Why do *I* have to wait? Have you ever found yourself asking the Lord this?

Waiting is especially difficult when it is something that your heart desperately longs for. Something that you know is good. Something that you believe is God's will. It can arouse a longing that comes from a depth that no one else knows about. A level so far down within our core that only God himself knows what resides at that depth of soul.

1. Lewis. *Mere Christianity.* 9.

96

The closer something is to our heart, the greater the struggle to wait for it. Or in my case, *her*. Our Vada. My Vada that, as I type this, is sitting in an orphanage on the other side of the globe. Our sweetheart that we don't know if her basic needs are being met like we would like for them to be. Our girl who is growing with each day that passes and . . . we are missing it. That hurts my mama heart. There is a massive ocean separating her and us. I would cross that ocean for her. And I intend to. This child that William and I have never met in person, *strangers made family*, by God himself. The God of the universe has bound us together, permanently. Just pictures emailed to us every month or two for now. Pictures that we stare at, study, and hold on to with all that we have. Pictures that, at this point, I look at once or twice, and then don't like to revisit because it is such a tangible reminder of the time, the person that I am missing . . . the growth that she is doing . . . the hugs and kisses I want to give . . . but can't. Pictures are nice, but they are not the real thing. They are only an image of the real thing. I want the real thing. *I want her.* I want her in my arms. I've wanted her in my arms since I was a child. Twenty years later, I stare at her face, and long for her.

We have never met. Our stories are very different, yet *God has chosen us* to be family. God has chosen her to be our daughter, and William and I to be her father and mother. We have each been chosen *for one other*. It's not something that any of us planned or predicted or manipulated to make happen. A simple "yes" on William and I's end, and a heart-breaking situation beyond her control on her end. Yet God has bound us together for life. How beautiful. How sacred. So, in a way, the waiting is sacred. *The waiting forces faith.* It forces dependence. It forces me to forfeit angst and frustration. It forces me to look to Jesus and rely on his plans . . . His plans for all of us. Psalm 37:7 reminds us "Be still before the Lord and wait patiently for him." Easier said than done. But hard was not foreign to the psalmist who penned this. God is ok with the hard. *He enters into the hard with us.* Amen. He is in this. He is orchestrating it. Building our family according to his will. So, I am choosing, even this day, to trust his timing. *An act of the will. A choice. A belief.*

I love her already. I am ecstatic to learn her. To know her, personally. To laugh at her facial expressions, something I can tell from her pictures are one of the many rich parts of her. She is expressive. To experience her personality. To enjoy her as she explores, learns, and plays. To hold her. To kiss her, incessantly. I ache for her. Is this how the Lord feels about us,

I wonder to myself? I am sitting in her future room as I type this. I am writing this chapter from the glider that my sister gave me as a hand-me-down from my nieces' nursery. We have been told that we can expect to go get her in the next three months. I have longed for her for years. And so, I suppose, waiting another few months is what we will do. We have no other choice. The bureaucracy and legality of this whole process is well beyond our control. But for a recovering control freak, take-the-bull-by-the-horns, make-it-happen personality, some days feel hopeless and drawn out. That is the nature of waiting, I suppose. But God, I believe, looks down on me with compassion, reminding me that, "he's got this." *Though the circumstances are beyond me, they are not beyond him.* And I am comforted, that is, when I am not too frustrated to listen. How about you? What waiting are you in? *He is there.* He is in it. He is compassionate towards your longing heart, dear one. Rest in his arms as you wait. He's got your situation. *He has you.*

My heart longs for all the children in Vada's orphanage to be adopted too. I am already having anxious feelings when I think ahead to the moment we get to take her from that orphanage to be ours forever. To go with us where we go, and have the last name Rackley transferred to her identity forever. I know my heart will be so full of joy, yet I am dreading the reality of seeing all the little faces, and soft cheeks, and eyes that will be left behind. Little ones who dream of having a family take them in as one of their own forever. I have to remind myself that those children are the Lord's and he will provide for them. But what can we, a community of Jesus followers, do to help them? Is the Lord calling you to make one of these precious children yours? Is he calling you to pray for them? To serve them in some capacity?

The truth is, if we could have had biological children, we likely wouldn't have the plans that we do to adopt more than one child, and we probably wouldn't be adopting at this time. I desperately want to be a mother to an adopted and biological child(ren). Vada needs a mother and a father. I am *so* glad he chose us to be hers. I see God's provision for my desire for adopted children. I see his provision for Vada's need for a family. Both our needs are being met. We need each other. And God, in his sovereignty and kindness, is weaving our needy stories together . . . in a really beautiful and healing way. He is forging the road ahead, and we are all the beneficiaries of his provision.

And so, we continue to wait for our precious Vada Tarike. Trusting that the Lord's timing is right. Trusting the Lord's provision for this child we have never met, across the ocean, who is our daughter. This child who I already feel so protective over, as she passes day after day, night after night in the orphanage. Trusting the Lord is providing the food, medical care and love she needs. Trusting the Lord is going to give her the power to heal from her brokenness. Trusting the Lord to give her joy and salvation. Trusting the Lord to grow our family as he sees fit. Trusting the Lord to flesh out his goodness to each of us as we walk forward not knowing what we are doing. Trusting the Lord is going to hold me in his grip until this process is completed. Trusting the Lord is going to give William and I wisdom to be first time parents to a child who was formerly orphaned. Trusting that he is able to speed up or slow down time as he sees fit. Trusting him to allow me to experience his power and love and provision in broken lives being redeemed, including, maybe even especially, my own. I am trusting him. He is all I have.

Isaiah 61:1-3 tells each of us that "he has sent me to bind up the brokenhearted, to proclaim freedom for the captives and release from darkness for the prisoners, to proclaim the year of the Lord's favor and the day of vengeance of our God, to comfort all who mourn, and provide for those who grieve in Zion—to bestow on them a crown of beauty instead of ashes, the oil of joy instead of mourning, and a garment of praise instead of a spirit of despair. They will be called oaks of righteousness, a planting of the Lord for the display of his splendor." (NIV) Amen. We are looking to you, in humble dependence, to do this in each one of our lives Lord.

CHAPTER 19

Steel Magnolia

"The question for us, then, is whether we trust in his power. And the problem for us is that in our culture we are tempted at every turn to trust in our own power instead. So the challenge for us is to live in such a way that we are radically dependent on and desperate for the power that only God can provide."

—DAVID PLATT[1]

There is a list of female writers who are Christians and have changed my life, each in her own way, and each for the better. Women like Katie Davis Majors, Corrie Ten Boon, Elisabeth Elliot, Joni Eareckson Tada, Mother Teresa, Kara Tippets, Sara Hagerty, Rebecca Deng and Korie Robertson. What is it about these ladies that inspires me so? Unmistakably, it's their deep and abiding love for Jesus. From that grows their drive to care for others. Their compassion for those in need. It is definitely their courage to go to the hard places and do the hard things. The unsafe places even, with joyful willingness. It is certainly their tenacity. Their grit when life is hard. It is their vision for the future. It is their sensitivity to see and care for the individual right in front of them. Their recognition of being a citizen of another world while living in the brokenness of this one. Oh, they inspire me! I see that it is Jesus inside of them that I am really longing for though. Jesus is who *I* am longing for. He himself is the reward. The reward that is

---

1. Platt. *Radical.* 45.

found in the hard places. It's not the healing, the dream fulfilled, the prayer answered . . . it's Jesus. *He is the reward.*

Women truly have a unique, unmatched opportunity to display the beauty of Jesus to the world. The compassion, tenderness, nurture and life infusing spirit that women can give to others is something special. Something coming straight from the hand of God. He has given this to women, alone, and it is a powerful gift. A gift that can infuse life, maybe physical, maybe otherwise, to another human being. A gift that is different from what a man can offer the world. And we intend to use this gift . . . to not let our pain and the lessons we have learned in the hard places to be wasted. It is one of my sole purposes for writing this book, a task Jesus asked me to do, and I was (and am, who am I kidding?) greatly intimidated at. I have prayed over every page, every word, that it might infuse *life to you,* dear sister. I wish I could sit *with you,* right now, over a warm mug of coffee, and listen to *your story* . . . I know you would infuse life to me too. Our stories are unique and powerful. It would be a shame to not generously share them with one another and grow together.

We so often learn when we are in hard places. Hard times. Hard situations. Lessons seem to stick better when we are in those moments, struggling, don't you think so? What hard time are you in right now? What lesson may the Lord be tenderly trying to show you in this season? Sometimes these days, when I am walking through a hard season, I pray, "Lord, don't let me miss what you have for me here." We can miss it so easily. We can fold our arms and pout in the corner if we decide to dig the heels of our heart into the ground, saying "No!" to the Lord. But though that reaction is tempting, it doesn't satisfy our souls like when we lift the palms of our heart up to the Lord, saying, "Show me! Show me, Lord, what it is that you are trying to teach me here!" That surrender to the Lord may come every day. Maybe every hour. Maybe every five minutes, depending on how difficult the situation is to us. *But with grit, and us pointing the eyes of our hearts Godward, that surrender can bring forth blooms that are the most vibrant of all the flowers in the garden.*

Have you ever experienced Jesus sitting with you in the dark? Not disappointed in you. Just sitting with you in your sorrow? There is so much wisdom to be learned in that place as you feel his strong arm tightly gripped around your shoulder and see his teardrop fall and wet the ground beside where you are both sitting. One good thing about suffering is that it teaches us how to tenderly and effectively care for others who are suffering. How has God used your suffering to be a blessing, a comfort to others? We all suffer. I once heard it said that suffering is not competitive. We all walk through hard things. It is a part of being human. And we *need* each other when we suffer. And *suffering looks different on all of us, but it is equally real.*

2 Corinthians 1:3-5 says, "Blessed be the God and Father of our Lord Jesus Christ, the Father of mercies and God of all comfort, who comforts us in all our affliction, so that we may be able to comfort those who are in any affliction, with the comfort with which we ourselves are comforted by God. For as we share abundantly in Christ's sufferings, so through Christ we share abundantly in comfort too." The idea being that from our grief experience, another person may benefit. We can comfort others the way we have experienced being comforted, tenderly and compassionately. The way Jesus cared for others, so we can care for one another. I have learned to not try to control someone else's grief. The better way is just to meet them where they are at. Just be with them. *There is so much power in presence.* No need to talk them out of it or help them try to "see on the bright side." Sometimes, there really is no bright side. So often words are not even needed. Sometimes they are, and it is good to speak into those moments. But often it is the quiet presence of another amid suffering that can cause love to speak the loudest.

I once heard the description of women who follow Jesus as "Steel Magnolias." Being from the south and loving the show "Fixer Upper," I do like magnolias. They smell beautifully, they are pretty to look at, and their giant green leaves make the perfect holiday decorations. But I don't just like the phrase steel magnolias because they are pretty flowers, or because I grew up watching the movie, or because my favorite reality TV show is trademarked by a magnolia tree being planted in the front yard by Chip and Johanna Gaines. I like the term steel magnolias for much more than that. It is the softness, beauty, purity, peacemaking qualities of a white magnolia flower that is femininity at its most lovely. Irresistibly attractive. A warmth in a cold world. A cashmere amongst the thorns. A shady oasis in the desert.

The strength, however, of steel is unbreakable, unshakeable and undeniable. It is grounded, firm, reliable, wise, sturdy and tough. It has grit. You cannot bring it down, and it can withstand the roughest conditions. It endures without wavering. A *Steel Magnolia* is such a powerful picture to me of a godly woman. The women that I have mentioned in this chapter are all steel magnolias. They have all given life to me, especially during some of my loneliest and heartsick days. I am grateful for and humbled by their influence.

This is the type of woman that I hope to be. This is the type of woman that I am praying for God to make me. This is the type of woman that I am praying God makes our precious Vada Tarike and any other daughters that may join our family in the future. I am learning God uses hard situations, things that make us weak, things that we really believe might break us, to create dependence. Therein, he enters. Therein real growth, noticeable blooming happens. Even though it is difficult to endure, *it shows his love of our souls at any and all costs.* This, to me, makes the trials a little easier to endure. I pray, dear friend, that this book encourages you to view your trials the same way. *To my dear, female readers . . . Hang on sister. Let's be steel magnolias together to the glory of God.* I pray that as your tears fall to the ground—may they be watering seeds that will bring forth vibrant, glorious blooms this spring.

CHAPTER 20

The Orphanage Gates

"But God gives life to the dead. He calls things that are not, as though they are."

—SARA HAGERTY[1]

My heart was pounding. I felt like my whole life had been preparing me for *this* moment. I had watched countless YouTube videos of others doing this . . . and now . . . *now* . . . here I was, about to meet my daughter face-to-face for the first time. On foreign soil, I scanned my eyes around and allowed my body to absorb all the different, sights, smells, and sounds around me as I wobbled in the backseat of the van down the streets that were taking me to her. Exhaust loomed heavy in the African air as it penetrated my nostrils. Pedestrians filled the busy streets carrying goods on their backs and heads to sell as we jetted in and out of the congested, city traffic. We pulled off main roads and began taking side streets filled with dogs, goats and lone pedestrians, "we must be getting closer," I thought anxiously to myself. I couldn't talk. I was too lost in thought. I was absorbing the moment, taking in the magnitude of what was happening with excitement and gratitude.

There it was, the orphanage sign, nothing much to look at. It was a small, rectangular shaped piece of tin, standing high above the dirt, pothole covered side street. It read "Sele Enat Mahiber." I knew we were here. I could hardly breathe. I had been longing for this moment for the past

1. Hagerty. *Every Bitter Thing.* 130.

twenty-three years. The van came to a stop, rocking me forward in my seat. The loud side door of the van swung open. I climbed out knowing I would be a different person when I got back in. My palms were sweating and my heart was racing. I gave a nervous, "this is happening grin" to Sammie, my translator, and Debra, my mother-in-law who had accompanied me on this unexpectant, leap-of-faith trip. I felt like I was watching someone else do this, but it wasn't someone else. It was me. I knew that just over those tin walls, my daughter was in there! The one I had been dreaming about, praying over, and the one my arms were aching to hold for the past fourteen months, or was it the past twenty-three years? I was now breathing the same air she was. I wasn't separated by an ocean anymore, just a thin piece of tin and a bored looking guard and friendly, tick-infested dog at the gate. The matted, sandy colored dog walked up and sniffed my ankles, surely sensing my nerves.

I gently shook my head to remind myself this was real. The moment felt so oddly quiet. The drive over was filled with noise from the bustling, capital streets of Addis Ababa, a city of seven million people, which never sleeps. Seven million people in this city, but I was here for one. The one. I looked down at my feet as I stood on mixed dirt and rubble-cracked concrete and took in the silence around me on this sleepy side-street. Sammie walked ahead, familiar with this scene. I followed him, thankful for his experience and confidence in this moment that felt so vulnerable and sacred.

William was at home, planning to come join me as soon as I got the last approval we needed to be given an official court date. We had been waiting for one piece of paper to arrive from fourteen hours away, near the Sudan border. One stinking piece of paper. "We" were having a lot (emphasis on a lot) of trouble getting it. I knew other aching heart, separated-from-their-children adoptive mamas in similar situations who had flown over without permission and were doing the same thing I was, fighting to get what we needed to bring our children home! When William found out what they were doing, and that many of their husbands also planned to join them once approval was obtained, he consented to let me go. I had gone over on an earnest prayer that my coming would help speed the process along. A process we were beginning to believe was being intentionally delayed for the benefit of some of the in-country staff's salaries. You see, Ethiopia passed a law *in the middle* of our adoption process stating that no more international adoptions would be allowed. We were over half way through the process and had been matched to Vada Tarike for months at that point. She was ours. And we were really scared that we were going to lose her, and not to a good situation. Another reason our faith was built by William's heart being changed when it was. If we had started the adoption, even two weeks after we did, we likely would have lost her. We knew many families whose adoptions fell through during this time, and we were terrified of losing our girl.

I was there to advocate for our daughter. William planned to come join me as soon as we got the green light. He was only allowed a few weeks off at work, and we knew he would have to be there during the legal part of the process. This is what four other families we knew had done and been successful with, so we did it too. An expensive risk, but does your child have a cost? He was at home, heart pounding too, knowing our daughter would soon be in my arms. So thankful I was there, but heartsick he couldn't be sharing in this moment too. Debra, my Jesus-loving mother-in-law accompanied me on the trip. Well acquainted with international travel, she insisted on being my travel buddy. I was thankful for her companionship on this emotionally tense battle ground that we were fighting to win with Vada.

I followed our translator, Sammie, through the winding orphanage compound. Winnie the Pooh was painted on the blue tin wall, and my heart smiled seeing the kindness it represented to the children. To my right, Tom and Jerry were painted on a concrete wall leading into a small cafeteria. I felt the uneven stones under my feet and my senses were on hyperalert as I followed Sammie into a small, nearly silent courtyard. Large, woven drapes hung through the courtyard on drying lines. I saw a small building ahead with pale yellow walls inside, the same yellow walls that served as the backdrop to all the pictures we had received of our girl. This is it. This is where she is I instinctively knew. I saw toddlers waddling around through the all glass, large front windows, stuffed animals scattered all over the floor.

My eyes scanned the faces. Wait, I immediately jolted my head back to the left, there she is! Our Vada Tarike! In real life! There she is! My heart jumped inside of my chest, and I immediately fell in love. I starred at her through the glass wall as she stood wedged between the couch and the wall, able to squeeze out if she wanted to, a tight spot she had found her busy-little-self into. Her eyes were big, espresso brown, just like her pictures. She locked eyes with me through the window. She noticed I was fixated on her. She doesn't miss a beat. I had a smile I couldn't wipe off my face. There she was, in real life, I was transfixed. After a few short seconds her image blurred because tears were welling in my eyes. There is my daughter. My beloved girl. I put my hand out against the glass window, taking in the moment. My heart soared and my tears fell to the Ethiopian ground. In that moment I realized, the last seven years had brought me to this very moment. Tear-watered blooms had given me my forever cherished Vada Tarike. She embodies our most adored bloom from this tear infested season. We were in Addis Ababa, on one of our drives to the orphanage I learned in Amharic (the national language of Ethiopia) Addis Ababa means "new flower." It all made sense. I took off my shoes to go inside.

Images

William always trying to make me laugh. One day while getting chemo he tied a scarf around his head and was making funny jokes to try and make me laugh. He is God's greatest gift to me.

Okra thief!

Garden goodness!

Cancer's gone party with friends from church. I'm on the far left. Each of these friends were so supportive during that painful season.

William got me this shirt and I wore it to all my follow up visits in the cancer center after the cancer was gone. It's still one of my favorite shirts today. Cancer really does suck!

Last day of radiation treatment!

Our dog, Daisy, playing with one of the horses!
She's a country dog at heart.

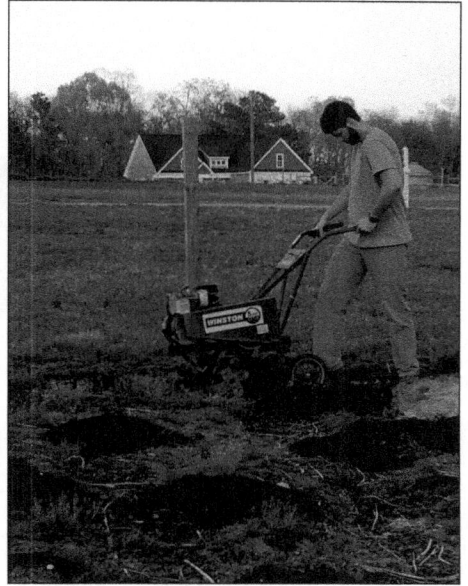

William tilling the garden at Pond Valley Lane.
A place that the Lord and I would wrestle in
prayer together.

Riding a camel with some of the children at Rafiki Village in Kenya. This was the
summer after my freshman year at University of North Carolina at Chapel Hill.

The best feeling I have ever experienced, such relief! Leaving the courthouse in Addis, we immediately got in the van to go to the orphanage to get our daughter!

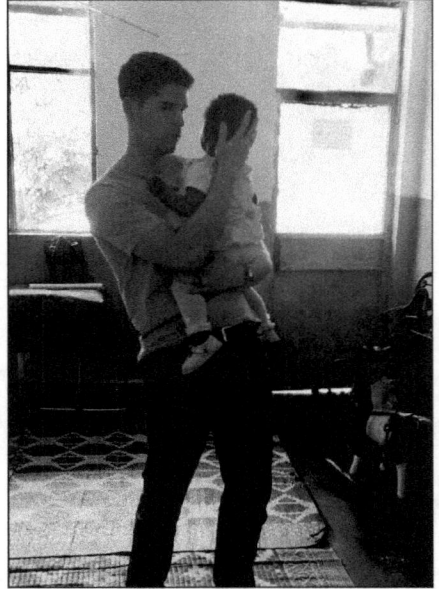

William's first time holding Vada. He describes it as pure relief. He said he wanted to heal all the pain she had ever been through. His protective daddy heart surfaced immediately. She is his girl.

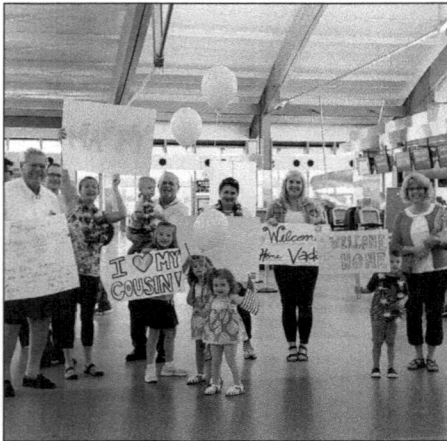

Our sweet family waiting to welcome us home from Ethiopia at the Raleigh-Durham International Airport!

My view from the front porch at Pond Valley Lane. This is where I spent a lot of time grieving and praying alone with the Lord as I watched the horses graze.

The orphanage sign. This mama heart has never been so happy to be anywhere ever before. I was so relieved to finally be with my girl.

Our favorite tear watered bloom. For months leading up to our adoption I prayed that God would give our child unexplainable joy. She is the most joy-filled soul I have ever known. Her excitement and humor add so much sunshine to our lives. To know her is to love her!

My favorite picture of all time! The first time I got to hold my daughter. I thought my heart literally might explode.

Our driver, Yeli, and translator, Sammie in Ethiopia! They were both so helpful and kind.

Waiting at the passport office in Addis! Lots of meetings and appointments to prepare to come home tuckered us all out, especially our sweet Vada Tarike.

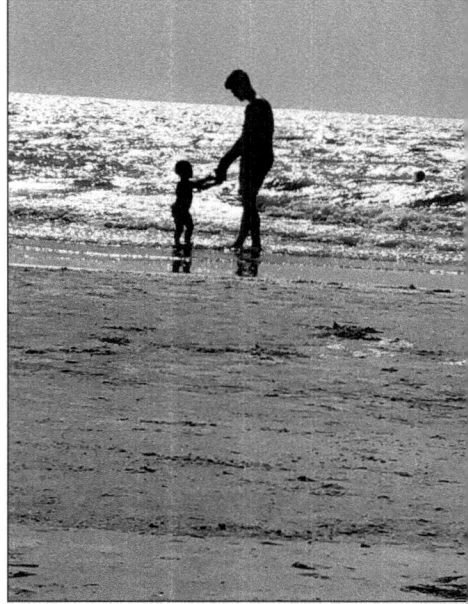

Daddy's girl.

Bibliography

Clark, Beth. *Kisses from Katie*. New York. Howard. 2011.

Davis, Katie. *Kisses from Katie*. New York. Howard. 2011.

Davis Majors, Katie. *Daring to Hope*. New York. Crown. 2017.

Demoss, Nancy. Kassian, Mary. *True Woman 201*. Illinois. Moody. 2015.

Elliot, Elisabeth. *Through Gates of Splendor*. New York. Harper & Brothers. 1957.

Hagerty, Sara. *Every Bitter Thing is Sweet*. Michigan. Zondervan. 2014.

Lewis, C.S. *Mere Christianity*. New York. Harper Collins. 2001.

Miller, Paul. *Love Walked Among Us*. Colorado. NavPress. 2014.

Platt, David. *Radical*. Colorado. Multnomah. 2010.

Tada, Joni Eareckson. *God's Hand in Our Hardship*. Massachusetts. Rose. 2012.

———. https://www.epm.org/blog/2016/Nov/7/joni-suffering-sorrow-wheelchairs.

Ten Boom, Corrie. *The Hiding Place*. New York. Bantam. 1974.